# MENSA

# MIGHTY

# MIND BOOSTERS

Metro Books
122 Fifth Avenue
New York, NY 10011

ISBN: 978-1-4351-1699-3

Printed and bound in Singapore

10 9 8 7 6 5 4 3 2 1

# MENSA®

# MIGHTY
# MIND BOOSTERS

**Robert Allen**
**Josephine Fulton**

METRO BOOKS
NEW YORK

# American Mensa® Ltd

American Mensa Ltd is an organization for individuals who have one common trait: an IQ in the top 2% of the nation. Over 57,000 current members have found out how smart they are. This leaves room for an additional 6 million members in America alone. You may be one of them.

Looking for intellectual stimulation?
If you enjoy mental exercise, you'll find lots of good "workout programs" in the *Mensa Bulletin*, our national magazine. Voice your opinion in one of the newsletters published by each of our 134 local chapters. Learn from the many books and publications that are available to you as a member.

Looking for social interaction?
Are you a "people person," or would you like to meet other people with whom you feel comfortable? Then come to our local meetings, parties, and get-togethers. Participate in our lectures and debates. Attend our regional events and national gatherings. There's something happening on the Mensa calendar almost daily. So, you have lots of opportunities to meet people, exchange ideas, and make interesting new friends.

Looking for others who share your special interest?
Whether yours is as common as crossword puzzles or as esoteric as Egyptology, there's a Mensa Special Interest Group (SIG) for it.

Take the challenge. Find out how smart you really are. Contact American Mensa Ltd today and ask for a free brochure. We enjoy adding new members and ideas to our high-IQ organization. For more information about American Mensa: www.us.mensa.org, or

American Mensa Ltd
1229 Corporate Drive West
Arlington, TX 76006-6103

Email: nationaloffice@americanmensa.org
Voicemail: 800/66/MENSA
Phone: 817/607/0060
Fax: 817/649/5232

# CONTENTS

# FOREWORD

This book is designed to challenge you in a number of ways. First, in an age when we are constantly being urged to improve our physical fitness, our mental faculties are taken for granted. Schools and colleges teach academic subjects while largely playing down issues such as how to learn, how to improve concentration, or how to conquer our fear of certain disciplines. This book aims to fill that gap.

The author, a statistician by training, has produced a number of tests that help self-assessment of our aptitude in vital areas, such as learning skills, concentration, numerical and verbal skills, decision making and creativity. Some of the tests, such as those that assess concentration, are intentionally very tough. After all, when you are in a situation where concentration counts, one slip could lead to disaster.

By practice and perseverance we can improve our mental powers. Sometimes things hold us back — for example, the common yet completely irrational fear of numbers. This book suggests a number of ways in which we can overcome such difficulties, and also offers hints and tips for improving performance. The message here is that we can change the way we are, and be better for it.

The second part of the book has another purpose. It is a test of your ability to think clearly. The problems set here will force you to grapple with a variety of situations that can only be resolved by the rigorous application of logic. Normally we think of logic as one of those dry and dusty subjects that lurks in the realms of mathematics and philosophy – but that need not be so. The problems you will find here are purely for fun and will keep you entertained while sharpening your wits.

*R. P. Allen*

Robert Allen

# MIND POWER CONTENTS

# Developing Learning Skills

Does the prospect of learning a foreign language or trying to master the latest piece of equipment at work fill you with apprehension? The first step in overcoming this is to develop confidence in yourself. Learning anything new often seems daunting, but telling yourself that you cannot possibly do it is the guaranteed route to failure.

If you think about the impressive range of skills that you possess, you will realize that it is only your own anxieties that are holding you back. The skills that you use from day to day may seem very ordinary, but in fact they represent a vast amount of knowledge that you have already taken in your stride. Answering the questions below should help to make you more aware of your enormous learning potential.

ASSESS YOURSELF

ASSESS YOURSELF (A)

# (A) ASSESS YOURSELF

1. Can you walk?

2. Can you talk?

3. Can you distinguish between different shapes/sounds/textures and so on?

4. Are you numerate and literate, even at the most elementary level?

5. Can you make a cup of coffee?

6. Can you cook?

7. If not, do you know how to order a takeaway?

8. Can you go out and buy a loaf of bread?

9. Can you cross the road safely?

10. Do you have a fairly clear idea of your likes and dislikes?

11. Can you communicate these to others?

12. Do you have any hobbies? Think about the skills, however basic, that you need for these.

13. Do you know any words of a foreign language?

14. Can you drive?

15. If not, are you familiar with other public or private means of getting around?

16. Have you ever taken on any kind of work, either paid or voluntary?

17. Are you familiar with any technological equipment, from telephones and hi-fis to the Internet?

18. Can you change a plug, or know who to contact if you can't?

19. Can you name 10 other countries?

20. Can you name the President of the USA?

These questions should have highlighted the wide range of skills and information that you have acquired since birth – simply surviving from day to day requires a continuous cycle of learning. Now turn to the following tests to give yourself an idea of just how good your learning abilities are.

# How Does it Work?

Study the instructions for the various imaginary gadgets listed below. After 10 minutes, turn the page and attempt the multiple-choice questions to discover how much information has registered.

## 1. The Ho-hum
To operate safely, only remove the protective shield when cutting is in progress. Align the heel at the appropriate foot-size mark and set the gender dial. When all is in place, raise the shield and activate the red button. The blue dial controls the degree of nail trim. Activating the green button switches the Ho-hum off, and automatically lowers the shield, after a 10-second period, to allow for foot removal.

## 2. The Didgerer
The Didgerer is not suitable for use in very confined spaces. To operate, aim the pointed end towards the animal, ideally within a distance of 12 feet to guarantee accuracy. Click the protruding end in, while still pointing toward the animal to activate the sensory device. Releasing the end at any time results in the catcher being automatically wound in. The Didgerer is effective with both still and moving creatures, with minimal trauma.

## 3. The Doodar
Switch the Doodar on after ensuring that all 5 batteries are correctly in place. Using the arrow keys, highlight the 6 adjectives characterizing your current mood from the Trait List appearing on screen. Finally, move the cursor to "All" to register your mood and to display a choice of aromatic remedies. After detailing your current location as prompted, a list of outlets supplying the aromatherapy oils is displayed, with details of stock levels. After use, simply switch off.

## 4. The Whatsitsname
Having produced your chosen culinary mixture, set the white Whatsitsname gauge to the switch that is relevant to the mixture, e.g. cake base, savoury sauce etc. Place the sterilized Whatsitsname into the mixture, and stir for 5 seconds. Remove and wipe to determine the exact amount of thickening agent (provided) required to produce the perfect consistency. Place in the sterilizer before further use in order to clean and reset the device.

## 5. The Heebie-jeeby
Using the suction pads, attach a Heebie-jeeby centrally on each window after leaving the vehicle during cold weather, particularly at night. Place the rectangular Heebie-jeebies on the front and rear windscreens, and the square Heebie-jeebies on the smaller side windows. To activate, turn the circular switch on each one clockwise until the arrow is level with the orange dot. Remove when using the vehicle, whose windows will be frost-free. When the switch is jammed towards the yellow dot, recharging is necessary.

ASSESS YOURSELF

ASSESS YOURSELF (A)

**ASSESS YOURSELF**

# Questions

**1** How many adjectives are used to describe your mood on the Doodar?
**a)** 8  **b)** 5  **c)** 6  **d)** 7  **e)** 4

**2** What gadget is used in connection with animals?
**a)** Whatsitsname  **b)** Heeby-jeeby  **c)** Ho-hum  **d)** Didgerer  **e)** Doodar

**3** What controls the degree of nail trim on one of the gadgets?
**a)** a blue button  **b)** a blue switch  **c)** a green switch  **d)** a blue dial  **e)** a green button

**4** Where should you not use the Didgerer?
**a)** in a car  **b)** in a ballroom  **c)** in a park  **d)** in a department store  **e)** on a mountain

**5** Which of the following is a named feature of the Ho-hum?
**a)** suction pads  **b)** protective shield  **c)** white gauge
**d)** battery-operated mechanism  **e)** sensory device

**6** What shape should the gadget that sits on the rear windscreen be?
**a)** circular  **b)** triangular  **c)** rectangular  **d)** square  **e)** irregular

**7** What is used to reset the Whatsitsname?
**a)** a cleanser  **b)** a dial  **c)** a white gauge  **d)** a green button  **e)** a sterilizer

**8** What must be detailed to register a list of outlets on one of the gadgets?
**a)** your current geographical location  **b)** your foot-size  **c)** your home address
**d)** your current mood  **e)** your car

**9** How should the switch on the Heeby-jeeby be activated?
**a)** pressed in  **b)** turned clockwise  **c)** clicked  **d)** pulled out  **e)** pushed up

**10** Within how many feet should the Didgerer be operated?
**a)** 6  **b)** 15  **c)** 8  **d)** 10  **e)** 12

# Finding the Right Words

Study this list of words and accompanying definitions for 5 minutes only – efficient learning is related to speed. Then turn the page, look at the two lists of definitions and words that follow, and match them up. Beware of the red herrings! The test definitions are worded differently from those in the first list, which means that the ability to learn and understand, and not just a good memory, are vital to do well. Of course, if you are already familiar with any of the words, you will have to account for this when scoring.

---

Lamellibranch: animal of the mollusc class

Eupepsia: good digestion

Afrormosia: African teaklike wood

Riparian: inhabiting or situated on a river bank

Nidifugous: (of birds) leaving their nest soon after being hatched

Imbroglio: confused state of affairs

Nagelfluh: Swiss or Italian conglomerate rock

Guaiacum: South-American tree whose components are medicinal

Now get matching!

---

**ASSESS YOURSELF**

**ASSESS YOURSELF**

**ASSESS YOURSELF**

ASSESS YOURSELF

## Definitions:

**1** Pertaining to a slope by water

**2** Hard, yellow-brown plant material

**3** Young fledgling active at an early age

**4** Soft-bodied animal with a hard shell

**5** Perplexing situation

**6** Large plant bearing therapeutic properties

**7** The satisfactory processing of food in the stomach

**8** European coarse-grained mineral matter

Pick out which of these words match the above definitions:

**A** Gualica

**B** Nagelfluh

**C** Imbroglio

**D** Samelibranch

**E** Afrormosia

**F** Eupepsicum

**G** Riparicer

**H** Imbragsia

**I** Nidifugous

**J** Bagelflew

**K** Riparian

**L** Eupepsia

**M** Lamellibranch

**N** Guaiacum

These kinds of tests give you a good general idea of your ability to learn, and yet they cannot tell the whole story. Learning is a complex process and your capacity to digest, retain and recall information is greatly influenced by the situation you find yourself in, and the way in which information is presented to you.

# Early Influences

Our ability and desire to learn stems predominantly from our childhood. Learning to walk and talk is largely a matter of mirroring and repetition, so the degree of encouragement and attention that you receive has a huge influence on your early progress. Anyone with a younger brother or sister will no doubt remember how annoyed they sometimes felt about being constantly copied. Only later in life do we realize just how valuable this learning process is.

From birth onwards, we learn through a continual cycle of habituation – getting used to something – and readjustment. A baby's initial encounter with anything new is often greeted with terror. Only reassurance and closer examination will reveal that the rocking horse, for example, really is harmless.

All of us have a deep-seated desire to question the world around us. As children, "why?" is a key word in our vocabulary. Unfortunately, the path of learning is too often blocked by other people's negative responses – what can any child learn from being told "because it does"? Criticism is equally harmful. If a child is told that his or her handwriting is dreadful, that child may well take this as a direct attack on their personality. This could seriously damage their confidence, and consequently dampen further motivation to learn. What is needed, for children and adults alike, is positive encouragement and

ways of teaching that clearly separate someone's personality from the skills they are trying to master. With this approach, our learning skills should flourish, from birth right through to our mature years.

There are other influences from our early years that affect our attitude toward learning in later life. Fond memories of being read to, or helped to read, at bedtime often means that reading is subconsciously linked with pleasure. This could be the start of a lifelong love of reading, which will undoubtedly help to make us more efficient learners.

**PUT IT IN PERSPECTIVE**  (P)

# What is Learning?

The information we take in when we are reading is stored in the many millions of cells that make up the human brain. These cells are connected by a vast network of pathways known as dentritic spines. Acquiring new knowledge doesn't mean that the brain gets too "full" and information is lost in some way – instead, it causes the brain to develop additional pathways. Put simply, the more you learn, the more you are able to learn.

Each of us learns in different ways. For example, ask a friend to observe you discretely at some point in the future when you are in the middle of a discussion. You must be unaware of this, so that you act in a perfectly natural way. How do your mannerisms and facial expressions change when you are asked a question, and when you are listening? What happens to your eyes?

Some people believe that close observation of how your eyes move when you are interacting with others can reveal the way in which you prefer to learn and process information. If your eyes dart upward when you are asked a question or are trying to remember something, you could be someone who responds well to visual images. This is thought to be because you are glancing toward the top of the head which, roughly speaking, is where the eyes are located. This tendency might be emphasized by a preference for using visual language, such as "let's see" and "my view is..." Visual learning can be highly effective because images are often much more appealing and accessible than words. When you pick up a newspaper, are your eyes instantly drawn to the opening paragraph of a story or the photograph that goes with it?

According to this theory, eyes darting to the side, toward the ears, can reflect a reliance on sound and hearing. Again, someone who responds well to sound may use language that reflects this: "I hear you..." "Sounds like a good idea" and so on. Sound is certainly important to all of us as we learn – the tone of a voice, as well as its modulation and volume, can make a huge difference to how we take in spoken information. Stress on one word rather than another could make all the difference to the message we are receiving from the speaker. Also, a narrative delivered with lively enthusiasm and using the full range of the voice is much more memorable than one spoken in flat, inexpressive tones – the ear as well as the mind must be stimulated to maintain your interest and optimize your learning capacity.

The other senses – taste, touch and smell – also play a vital role in our learning processes. Schools and colleges now place great emphasis on active self-discovery, using the full range of the senses, as opposed to relying on passive reading. Recollection of information or past experiences can often be triggered through a familiar smell or taste rather than words.

Think about how you, as an individual, rely on your senses to learn. What sort of language do you use or respond well to? Perhaps you would like to "chew this over" or the answer may be "on the tip of your tongue". Hopefully, you don't "smell a rat". Being aware of the learning potential that your senses offer can not only intensify your powers of understanding, but give your life another fascinating and enjoyable dimension, too.

**PUT IT IN PERSPECTIVE**

In the final analysis, you alone control your ability and desire to learn. Advice from others is all very well, but unless you make an effort to use it, no one can help you. The tips on learning technique outlined below are largely a matter of common sense, yet many people completely overlook them. Take the plunge and decide to review your current method of learning now – you might discover that you are missing out on all kinds of learning opportunities.

# Tips for Positive Thinking

**Your state of mind** dictates your ability to learn and succeed. If you tell yourself that you can't do something, the chances are you won't be able to. Instead of imposing these restrictions on yourself, think positive and focus on what you can do.

**Try treating your brain as a sophisticated filing cabinet,** containing positive and negative files. If you have a problem with numbers, for example, try shifting this mentally from a negative to a positive file. You will find that this can alter all kinds of subconscious preconceptions and totally alter the way you view your skills.

**Always stress what you have got right,** rather than what went wrong. This encourages a positive outlook and a heightened desire to know more. Everybody makes mistakes, but realizing how much you have learned in order to get as far as you have can boost your confidence and keep you going through the most difficult of situations.

**Learn from your mistakes.** Dejection is much more likely to set in if your mistakes always prompt feelings of failure rather than providing springboards for further progress. Work through your errors and try to gain something from them – don't give up and start resorting to wild guesses that will teach you nothing.

**The way in which you deal with the past, present and future** is a vital area of learning. Learning is much easier if you try to connect new information with past experience. When trying to remember a date, for instance, associating the numbers with those of a particular birthday or house number may prove invaluable. In this way, fresh information complements your existing store of knowledge rather than becoming a new file in the brain that is inevitably harder to locate.

**Use visualization techniques** to help you take on new information with greater ease. Try imagining yourself standing in the middle of a long road. Your past knowledge stretches away behind you, and the way ahead – your future learning path – is totally uncluttered.

**The sky's the limit.** Success is not limited – you need to recognize that you can never learn too much. The opportunities are always there, just waiting to be grasped.

**No one else can help you if you don't help yourself.** If you're confused about something, say so! Coming clean early on could prevent all kinds of complex problems and embarrassment later on.

**Take notice of what makes other people succeed.** Do you have a real problem with complicated calculations, for example, whereas your colleague manages them with ease? Instead of simply feeling resentful, try and find out how they approach the task. Some people believe that if you go even further and imitate some of the mannerisms and attitudes of that person, you can begin to get under their skin and so excel in the same areas. Your life cannot be a constant act, however – use the experience to question where you are going wrong and to get yourself on the right path.

TEST IT OUT

**TEST IT OUT** T

**Reinforcement is sure to improve your powers of retention.** This can mean questioning and participation, reading around a certain subject to add to your understanding, reviewing your knowledge at regular intervals, drawing up effective revision plans, and so on. Revision plans should be viewed as a fundamental part of an effective course of learning. When reading, a continual cycle of skimming, questioning, note-taking and recall testing is guaranteed to produce results to be proud of. The more time you spend planting an idea in your head, the harder it will be to uproot it.

**Reading and writing are not the only ways to learn and remember.** Look and listen carefully to everything around you. Use visual images if you respond well to those – a visual image of a lecturer in action can often trigger information you thought was lost. This does mean, however, that you need to watch and listen carefully to the lecturer in the first place!

**Be creative.** Play around with ideas by creating poems, sketches, and songs around the subject-matter in question. Nurture your creativity. Because it is so valuable in helping you to stay interested in a subject, it may repay you with interest.

**Experiment with music for the mind.** While many prefer to study information in silence, some people say that certain types of music actually help them to learn – which type is up to you to discover. You may well find that it helps your concentration as well as increasing your enjoyment of the learning process.

**Give yourself a break.** If you study from dawn until dusk, your interest will wane, and your learning ability will start to slow down. Try to maintain a balanced lifestyle, and keep your course of learning in perspective. Learn to take regular breaks and vary your environment – try a 5-minute walk around the garden. Constant study may well nourish your conscience, but your mind, like your body, is not programmed for endless exercise, and needs a chance to draw breath every now and again.

**Establish the learning environment that is best for you.** Some people thrive on early morning study, while others cannot even pick up a book until the evening. Experiment a little and discover your best learning environment – the hour, day or place that brings out the best in you. This may also encourage you to feel at ease with the prospect of learning, which is always beneficial.

**When you can find an interesting or amusing slant to something,** you are much more likely to take it in. Making learning stimulating and entertaining helps maximize your motivation and achievement.

 **Feel good about life, your health and learning,** and your performance will follow. Look after your body, and your brain will perform much better. You are in the driving seat, and all kinds of learning opportunities are waiting just around the corner. The speed with which you reach them is up to you.

## How Does it Work?

**Answers**
1.c   2.d   3.d   4.a   5.b
6.c   7.e   8.a   9.b   10.e

**Your score**
6 or less correct: Poor. Don't be discouraged – this is the kind of skill that can easily be improved.

7 or 8 correct: Good. Having a look at a few alternative learning techniques could improve your performance even more.

9 or 10 correct: Excellent. You have highly tuned talents where learning and recall are concerned. You might still benefit from looking at different learning strategies, however.

## Finding The Right Words

**Answers**
1K.   2E.   3I.   4M.   5C.   6N.   7L.   8B.

**Your Score.**
4 or below: Needs improvement.

5 or 6 correct: Good.

7 or 8 correct: Excellent.

**ASSESS YOURSELF**

# Maximize Your Memory

An efficient memory can add so much to your life, and yet many people simply say things like, "Oh, don't ask me, I can never remember a thing" and do nothing to make matters better. The following tests will help you to identify your position on the memory scale, pinpointing specific areas for self-improvement.

Use the following questionnaire to get a good general impression of how well your memory performs on a day-to-day basis.

---

## Scoring

Circle the number that you consider to be most appropriate: circle 1 if the statement definitely applies to you; 2 if this is the case sometimes, or you aren't quite sure; 3 if this is never the case.

1. When bumping into a long-lost acquaintance in the street, I can rarely remember his or her name.

    1    2    3

2. I tend to forget people's birthdays if I don't have some kind of written reminder.

    1    2    3

3. When reading a book, I can quite easily forget what I've just read in the previous chapter.

    1    2    3

4. Food shopping without a list often means that I end up having to make extra trips to the store.

    1    2    3

5. I have been guilty of forgetting to pass on vital phone messages.

    1    2    3

6. I often rely on other people to remind me to do a particular thing.

    1    2    3

7. It seems to take me ages to master any new words or foreign phrases.

                    1   2   3

8. It's unlikely that I would be able to remember a phone number if someone said it to me on the spur of the moment.

                    1   2   3

9. After being distracted in mid-conversation, I sometimes find myself asking what I was talking about before I was interrupted.

                    1   2   3

10. When it comes to following instructions for a recipe or a complicated gadget, I need to refer to them even after I've cooked the dish or used the gadget several times.

                    1   2   3

11. I have a tendency to forget either to watch a specific TV programme or to set the VCR for something I wanted to see.

                    1   2   3

12. I have burned food before now simply because I forgot it was in the oven.

                    1   2   3

13. Occasionally, I have waited ages for the kettle to boil and then realized that I have forgotten to switch it on.

                    1   2   3

14. I sometimes over-sleep when I have failed to set the alarm clock.

                    1   2   3

15. I have been known to turn up at a class or at work, having left an important document at home.

                    1   2   3

16. When I have stored something valuable in a "safe" place, it sometimes takes me a long time to hunt it out again.

                    1   2   3

17. If I'm taking some medicine, there will be times when I find myself wondering whether or not I have actually taken it.

                    1   2   3

18. I have sometimes totally forgotten to make a vital phone call.

                    1   2   3

19. I have trouble remembering which key is which when I'm carrying quite a few around with me.

                    1   2   3

20. I rarely remember what I've spent all my money on.

                    1   2   3

**ASSESS YOURSELF**

**ASSESS YOURSELF** Ⓐ

**ASSESS YOURSELF**

# Number Memory

In a world dominated by advanced telecommunications, and the many numerical codes that go with this, a good memory for numbers can make your life a whole lot easier. Test your short-term number memory by reading each of the following lines of digits aloud once, then turning away to write the numbers down in the same order.

---

## Scoring

For each line, see how many digits in a row you manage to remember correctly before making a mistake. When you get to the longer lines of numbers, see what your average score is (a score of 5 equals 5 numbers in a row remembered correctly).

| | | | | | | | | | | |
|---|---|---|---|---|---|---|---|---|---|---|
| 5 | | | | | | | | | | |
| 3 | 1 | | | | | | | | | |
| 3 | 9 | 4 | | | | | | | | |
| 7 | 2 | 8 | 9 | | | | | | | |
| 3 | 1 | 0 | 8 | 6 | | | | | | |
| 6 | 1 | 8 | 7 | 3 | 1 | | | | | |
| 1 | 0 | 4 | 7 | 9 | 2 | 4 | | | | |
| 9 | 8 | 7 | 1 | 4 | 3 | 8 | 9 | | | |
| 5 | 7 | 9 | 4 | 8 | 9 | 1 | 6 | 0 | | |
| 1 | 7 | 8 | 6 | 9 | 7 | 3 | 8 | 7 | 5 | |

# Visual Memory

Images can often be stored away in the memory and recalled much more efficiently than numbers or words. This is particularly true if the images are related in some way. Study these objects, all of which have something to do with the head or face, for 1 minute. Now turn the book over and make a list of the objects you can recall.

# Putting Names to Faces

Have you ever had the uncomfortable experience of bluffing your way through a chance meeting in the street with someone whose identity has completely eluded you? If so, you will know only too well that remembering a visual image is often of little use unless you can put a name to it. See how well you do when trying to remember the names and occupations of the following 12 uniformed people. You have two minutes before covering this box up, turning to the anonymous faces on the right, and seeing if you can give their identities back to them.

Mr Hazlewood, nurse  Ms Stacy, police officer  Ms Dupont, deep-sea diver  Mr Sorenson, carpenter

Ms Bukowski, firefighter  Mr Bergman, surgeon  Ms Harris, tennis player  Mr Gibson, office worker

Ms O'Riordon, violinist  Ms Brady, mechanic  Mr Rankin, artist  Ms Williamsburg, chef

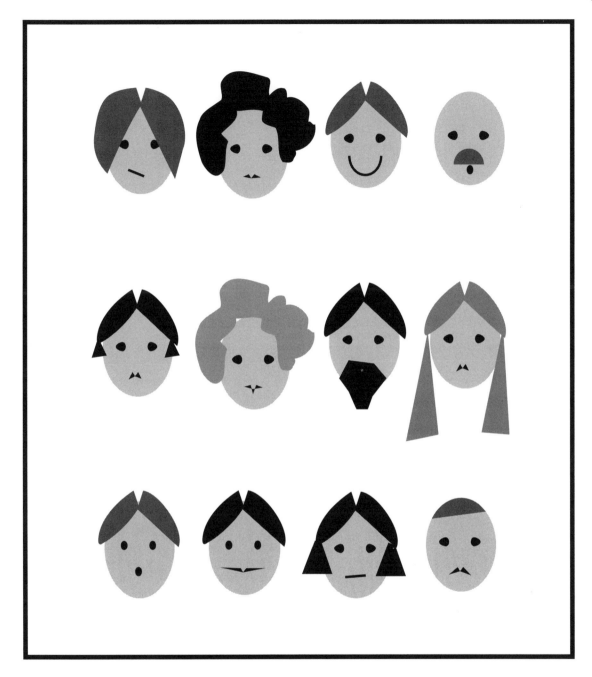

## Scoring

Score 2 for each person for whom you gave both the correct name and occupation, 1 if you got either one or the other correct, and 0 if you got neither correct. You will soon discover just how much easier visual images can be to recall than names.

> ## I have a photographic memory, but just occasionally I forget to take off the lens cap
> (anon – joke)

When you say "Oh dear, I've completely forgotten" about something, you might think that whatever it is you've forgotten is no longer stored in your memory and is lost forever. This is not the case. An inefficient memory is much more likely to be caused by an inability to recall things, rather than a failure to retain the information in the first place.

To take just a couple of examples, have extremely precise details and images from long ago suddenly burst into your consciousness, although they seemed lost for years? Or has a dream ever unexpectedly come to mind? A vast mass of information is locked away in your memory – all you have to do is find the key.

# Where does memory come from?

It seems that memory is not exclusively connected with one particular part of the brain. Because of the countless links between the huge numbers of brain cells, memory processes are constantly taking place all over this remarkable organ. More specific types of memory are, however, thought to spring from specific regions of the brain. An area called the limbic system, for example, is thought to have strong links with the way in which we record and recall general impressions. This is also the region that controls raw emotion, sex drive and appetite. Short-term memory, which lasts up to about 30 seconds, appears to be controlled by the temporal lobes on each side of the brain, while the parietal lobes behind the ears seem to be responsible for retaining knowledge of simple tasks. Visual memory occurs in the occipital lobes at the rear of the brain.

What this means is that serious damage to any of these regions of the brain can have severe consequences for the memory. In one case, a man whose temporal lobes had been badly damaged by an accident was left unable to recall the details of any recent events. Keeping up with the plot of a movie or simply knowing where he had been just a few hours previously became impossible tasks. So next time you complain about how poor your memory is, think again!

# A question of age

Age is directly related to memory skills, so there is little point in comparing the memory of a nine- and a ninety-year-old. For example, as young children, our frontal lobes, which are linked to the way we use language, are not yet fully developed. This means that a child's ability to distinguish between fact and fiction and to remember things accurately is also under-developed. How many times must this have been at the root of arguments between siblings, each convinced of their own version of a family saga? Just talking about things often helps to clear up some of these kinds of discrepancies, because verbal stimulation can trigger all kinds of memories.

At the other end of the scale, memory is said to deteriorate with age. But if you consider how many more memories seventy-year-olds have to contend with compared to their young grandchildren, it's hardly surprising that a few fall by the wayside! This may well be the result of a "last-in, first-out" principle: with new information constantly overlapping old, early memories are frequently the memorable. It's easy enough to recall the last meal you ate, but could you remember what you had for lunch exactly a month ago today?

There is encouraging evidence that older people today have far more efficient memories than their counterparts in previous generations. The sheer potential of the memory has been hugely underestimated in the past – now each year brings new scientific insights into the workings of the brain and memory, and there seems to be no limit to what can be achieved.

**PUT IT IN PERSPECTIVE**

**PUT IT IN PERSPECTIVE**

# Remembering ... and forgetting

Apart from age, there are many other factors that affect memory – not least of which is information overload. The continual barrage of new information that many of us face every day will inevitably affect the amount of knowledge to which we have instant access. Learning something fresh is never easy when your head is full of all kinds of other information. What is needed to overcome this problem is an organized, firmly focused mind.

Remembering is not the sole function of an efficient memory – much of what we "forget" also plays a vital role in our lives. If we were able to recall every single piece of trivia, from the exact dialogue of every conversation we have ever had to the precise ingredients of every meal we have eaten, then locating important bits of information would be a superhuman task. The extremely selective nature of the memory not only smooths our path in life, but it also interprets the past in a manner that fits in with our desires. This "editing" effect has both good and bad consequences. On one hand, it means that unpleasant memories can be wiped, which may often be a good thing. On the other hand, it means that events can be grossly distorted. This is why it is essential to talk about shared memories with other people, in order to stay as objective as possible.

# Giving yourself a prompt

Just as conversation can cause memories to come flooding back, so can specific circumstances or events, whether these are related to sight, smell or sound. Forgotten details can often be unlocked by making a return visit to a relevant environment. Obviously, if you want to jolt memories of a trip around the world, this method might not be feasible, but if you left your keys somewhere while out shopping, retracing your steps may prove invaluable.

As we've already mentioned in the learning chapter, it may be that the eyes play an important role in revealing how we recall events. Some research suggests that people's eyes immediately dart upward, downward, to the left or to the right when asked to recall matters that they connect strongly with their hearing, sight or touch. Darting in one particular direction could mean

that the memories in question relate to a specific sense – looking sideways, towards the ears, for example, may indicate the auditory sense. Like the different ways of learning that we've already looked at, an efficient memory often stems from making full use of all of the senses.

# The three major ways of learning and remembering are:

| REPETITION | ASSOCIATION | VISUALIZATION |

## Repeating Yourself Yourself Yourself

Simple repetition is not always enough for really effective learning and recollection, and repeating things over and over is not calculated to fill most people with enthusiasm. Repetition tends to produce effective recall only where simpler tasks are concerned. For more complex ones, properly organized memorizing is needed. Various techniques can be used. For example, the ability to recall written information is helped greatly by note-taking and by regular reviews – after half an hour, a day, a month.

# The Art of Association

When it comes to everyday life, and the need to remember a friend's phone number or what to buy at the supermarket, it's time to turn to a more approachable method – mnemonics. Mnemonics are simple, effective tricks to improve your memory, while stimulating your creativity at the same time. Repeating a phone number in your head because you don't have a pen with you could serve you well until you get home and write it down, but what are your chances of recalling the same number a week or month later without any other aid? Instead, try the following mnemonic method. Form a sentence by picking a word to represent each digit. The word should have the same number of letters as the digit it represents. For example:

The number **346443** could be remembered as

### "all (3 letters) good (4) things (6) take (4) time (4) too (3)."

Try remembering the reference number **B437 FEM**, a mix of numbers and letters, with:

### "Bedraggled (B) ants (4) ate (3) eagerly (7) for (F) eight (E) minutes (M)."

This method of association is easy to master – the more you do it, the easier it becomes. You will also find it an entertaining way of expanding your creative skills.

TEST IT OUT

**TEST IT OUT** T

# Using your visualizing skills

Images are also excellent memory aids. A written diary could become a thing of the past if more people developed the various tried and tested visual mnemonic techniques. Try remembering specific objects or events by placing them within a familiar visual context. For example, you might need to remember to find out about booking a trip abroad. Now imagine a walk through a very familiar place – your home or the local park, for example. As you go, insert images of relevant items – a wallet might remind you to work out how much foreign currency you need for your trip.

This method is an excellent one for remembering a list of objects or a sequence of events – from a shopping list to the step-by-step procedure for converting one program to another on your computer. You could try making the first thing that you pass on your route the most important item or event. Or perhaps the order of the images might mirror the chronological order of the events you are trying to memorize. In this way, the schedule for your week ahead might be committed to memory by a mental walk around your garden. Visualize a computer sinking beneath the waters of your pond (finish that vital report); a casket overflowing with coins under the oak tree (chase up unpaid invoices); a huge conductor's baton in the vegetable patch with tomato plants growing up it (a concert outing one evening), and so on...

The surroundings should remain unchanged, only the images you have inserted in order to remind you of something must be new. Ideally, the same scene with the same route should be used for every list you ever want to keep in your mind – with frequent use, remembering lists will become automatic.

If you make the added items and their position within your scenario obscure, out of place or amusing, they will linger in your memory much longer. The image of a giant fish, wearing sunglasses and relaxing happily in your bath, would make you much more likely to remember to buy that fish tank!

## Playing the system

You can begin to see just how effective systematic memory methods can be. Look at the letter triangle below. Read it through as if it were normal text, then cover it up and try to reproduce it yourself.

```
S
T  N
A  H  P
E  L  E  Y
T  N  I  A  D
```

Rather than storing information in countless single pieces, and laboriously fighting through them all in search of what you need, storing chunks of information enables quicker, more efficient access. Remembering two words is far easier than recalling 15 separate and seemingly random letters. Just as documents can be rapidly retrieved from a filing cabinet divided into a logical sequence of ordered sections, so information be recalled more easily from a well-structured memory. Of course one person will use a different filing system to another – test yourself to discover what works best for you.

# Recalling written material

Being able to retain and recall text is a vital skill for school, college, work and hobbies. Yet most people fail to organize the way in which they read and run the risk of losing up to 80% of the information after just 24 hours. So resolve to follow the BARCS system next time you want to be able to recall something you are reading:

## Breaks:

Have frequent short breaks between intensive periods of study, preferably after 45 minutes to an hour. Try to break for about 15 mins if you can, but any break is better than none. View this as a necessity, not an indulgence.

## Activity:

The memory performs much more efficiently if you approach reading actively. Take notes, read aloud, walk around the garden with the text – anything to help focus your attention.

## Reviews:

Review your previous learning session after each break – just take a couple of minutes to note down what you can remember.

## Comparisons:

Compare your notes with the original text. Any errors or omissions will be drilled further into your memory.

## Strengthen:

Spend a few minutes reinforcing the summarized material – a day later, a week later and a month later. You should find that much of this information will stay at your fingertips for a long time.

Your reading skills are closely intertwined with your powers of retention. If you learn to retain things more efficiently, you will find yourself reading faster, and focusing your attention more intensely. And time may be of the essence – for a student, less time spent reading means more time for valuable revision. Reading skills are examined in more depth later on (see pages 42–56).

TEST IT OUT

**TEST IT OUT**

# Pay Attention, But Enjoy Yourself Too

Failure to remember things cannot simply be attributed to a poor memory. Recollection may be impossible because the information simply wasn't absorbed and retained in the first place. Fundamental to an efficient memory is the ability to pay attention – if your mind wanders off to distant places while you are being told how to use a new computer, how can you even expect to remember how to turn the machine on?

Learn to concentrate on important details. When meeting new business clients, repeat their names over and over silently to yourself, making a mental note of any helpful associations. You might meet a Ms Redland, and remember her name because she has quite a reddish, ruddy complexion. Distinctive characteristics serve as great memory aids – as ever, the sillier, the better!

Improving your memory can be fun, and you can achieve astonishingly impressive results very quickly. Party games demanding the rapid memorizing of a tray of objects is quite literally child's play – making up a story that links the apparently unconnected items lodges them firmly in the memory. Some people can "magically" memorize the exact order of an entire pack of playing cards. The method, however, is simple: give the cards identities that you can then link up in the correct sequence. Perhaps you might like to remember each card as a member of a couple of sports teams, for example. Again, it's simply a matter of bundling together disparate images to form a collective group.

Rhymes can also prove to be highly entertaining memory-joggers. Just think of the children's rhymes that you sang years ago, yet can still remember. You could well find that your rhyming experiments render written lists unnecessary. Either compose your own little ditties, full of relevant references, or use a predetermined list of significant words. For this, try assigning a word to each letter of your name. If your name was Jane, this might be jumper for J, apple for A, and so on. Now try to connect each item on the list to each of these words in some way and create your rhyme. You can have a lot of fun making up really bizarre rhymes, but you will need to imprint jumper, apple etc on your memory – remember to remember!

# The Role of Your Subconscious

Your subconscious plays a huge role in influencing what you can and cannot remember. Anything your mind connects with fear and unease is guaranteed to impair performance – it's highly likely that at least once in your life you have emerged from a long-dreaded examination of some sort feeling really stupid because you forgot a basic fact or theory. Try to spend time relaxing and preparing yourself mentally for any stressful situations that require a healthily functioning memory. Pinpointing the cause of your fear should enable you to tackle it positively and leave your memory free of unnecessary hindrances. Adequate preparation will help to ensure that any fear is minimized, and your performance maximized.

As with everything, practice makes perfect – your memory will not improve unless you work at it. Shopping lists may serve as a reminder when you get to the supermarket, but you must remember to take the list along in the first place! The memory tips outlined in this section will become second nature if you make a little time to tackle them properly. You will then be able to trust your memory as much as it deserves. People often say, rightly, that the brain is far more intricate than any computer, so, unless you use and service it regularly, you can never get the most from it.

# See For Yourself

Assuming that you have remembered what you have just read, your memory should already be able to put into practice some of what it has learned. Tackling the tests below will show you how straightforward the memory techniques outlined above really are, while giving you an opportunity to devise simple methods of your own. The omission of a scoring system here is deliberate – you have already established how effective your basic memory skills are.
This is only the start of a promising future for your memory. Soon, your improved performance will say it all.

# Spot the Difference

Try tackling this game of spot the difference. First cover up the picture below on the right. Your task is to study the picture on the left for no more than 1 minute, trying to absorb every detail. Now cover the one on the left and look at the slightly different version on the right. What are the differences? There is no time limit, but your short-term memory deteriorates with time so the differences are unlikely to seem so obvious after a minute or two.

# Memorizing a List – Against the Clock

Now imagine that you've discovered an antique trunk full of all kinds of objects, in the depths of a wild forest. It has obviously been hidden there, undiscovered, for decades. You suddenly notice that, in your excitement, you have lagged far behind your companions, and desperately try to memorize the collection so that you can relate what you saw when you finally catch up. You know that you only have a couple of minutes to spare, or you will lose your friends completely, so concentrate, and see what you can remember after the five minutes that it will take you to rejoin your crowd.

# Number-crunching

Spend two minutes studying the table of numbers below before covering it up and trying to reproduce it yourself. Remember that simple repetition techniques may not be sufficient to help you.

| 2 | 6 | 6 | 1 |
|---|---|---|---|
| 3 | 4 | 2 | 6 |
| 6 | 3 | 6 | 0 |
| 4 | 2 | 1 | 8 |

# Self-assessment quiz

**Your score:**
20-33 Your memory seems to be letting you down, and could well benefit from some of the advice offered later on. For example, try using written reminders as a back-up aid. Perhaps it is actually your lifestyle that is to blame. Your life may be so hectic that you are simply placing too much strain on your poor old memory.
34-47 You appear to have a fairly reliable memory, with the occasional lapse from time to time. Learning a few useful techniques will help to heighten your memory skills further, especially when it comes to remembering things with greater accuracy.
48-60 Congratulations – your memory is in pretty good shape. You seldom forget things, perhaps largely as a result of a well-organized lifestyle. Read on to identify any more specific deficiencies, and to find out how you can improve your memory power even further.

# Number Memory

**Your score (for the longer number lines)**

1-4 Poor. Although you are below average now, however, there is plenty you can do to raise your scores.

5-7 Average. Your number memory is very much like most people's – which means that there's room for a little improvement.

8-10 Outstanding. Your short-term numerical memory serves you very well. Perhaps it's time to look at other areas of your memory skills, such as your visual memory.

# Visual Memory

Objects connected with the head and face

**Your score:**
1-7 Poor. The memory aids detailed later on will point you in the right direction.

8-10 Average. Your visual memory is pretty efficient, but you can still benefit from further practice.

11-12 Outstanding. Your visual memory is a major asset.

## Playing the System

It is unlikely that you met with much success. But careful study reveals that the words "dainty elephants" are trapped in the triangle as you read right to left, starting from the bottom right. Reproducing the letter triangle now is no problem.

## Memorizing a list – against the clock

Possible memorizing methods include the mnemonic system of moving through a scene; use of rhyme, although time is limited; and attaching words or images to the items.

## Number Crunching

Suggested memorizing method: the diagonals read 2, 4, 6, 8 and 1, 2, 3, 4; there is a double 6 in the top row and a 6 on either side. Now just fill in the gaps so that each column adds up to 15.

## Putting Names to Faces

**Your score**

0-13 Poor. You need to work through a few memory tips and techniques in order to exploit your potential.

14-20 Good. Keep working on your memory skills to improve even further.

21-24 Excellent. Your memory seems to cope pretty well with the tricky combination of word lists and visual images.

## Spot the Difference

1 Swimming costume on child was striped in left picture, but spotty right
2 Bucket is missing
3 Mum's sunglasses have been removed
4 One less boat is visible on the water
5 The windsurfer has no board
6 Part of the sandcastle is missing
7 The prominent cloud on the left is a different shape
8 The pattern on the beach-towel has changed
9 The fair-haired child now has dark hair
10 Dad was sitting on deckchair; he is now sitting on a sun-lounger
11 The waves are now capped with white foam
12 The vehicle pulled up at the back of the beach is different on right

You may not find it useful to apply any particular method here – instead, try focusing your attention by describing the images out loud or connecting individual features with past experience or even certain words. Hopefully, you will feel that your visual memory has a new heightened awareness.

# Reading Skills

Without basic literacy, everyday life can turn into a series of insurmountable hurdles. Having a strong command of language and reading skills unlocks the gate to a much more stimulating and rewarding world. Read on to see how you fare.

## Test Your Wordpower

Find the definitions that most closely correspond to the following words.

**1 polemic**
a. having electric charges
b. extreme cold
c. controversial
d. at a height

**2 fardel**
a. agricultural tool
b. burden
c. remote place
d. obese

**3 objurgate**
a. reprimand
b. cancel
c. replace
d. urge

**4 extemporaneous**
a. done without preparation
b. at the same time as
c. temporary
d. done in advance

**5 pilose**
a. criminal activity
b. drug addiction
c. covered with hair
d. cheerful

**6 juvenescence**
a. period of study
b. composition
c. state of complete elation
d. immaturity

**7 voluble**
a. talkative
b. gullible
c. generous
d. overflowing

**8 julep**
a. member of the mint family
b. type of drink
c. encouragement
d. children's game

**9 anneal**
a. heat metal or glass to toughen it
b. treat wound
c. apply protective covering
d. make member of a royal order

**10 oleaginous**
a. prehistoric
b. shiny
c. deceitful
d. oily or greasy

**11 lustrate**
   a. add extra diagrams
   b. perform ritual purification
   c. robust fitness
   d. enthuse

**12 unguent**
   a. stilted and hesitant
   b. ointment
   c. African hunter
   d. strong adhesive

**13 brio**
   a. rivalry
   b. the "spirit of the age"
   c. verve and vivacity
   d. arrogance

**14 cabochon**
   a. rank in the French army
   b. type of wheel common in
      ceremonial carriages
   c. polished gem without facets
   d. clever trick

**15 cicerone**
   a. person lacking courage
   b. conductor of sightseers
   c. heat-loving insect
   d. ancient temple

**16 rondo**
   a. piece of music
   b. Italian pasta dish
   c. lively dance
   d. poem of 10 or 13 lines

**17 tamarin**
   a. evergreen tree
   b. musical instrument
   c. tropical fruit
   d. South American monkey

**18 mettle**
   a. conductor of heat
   b. courage
   c. interfere
   d. weld together

**19 sibilant**
   a. with a hissing sound
   b. close family relation
   c. family reunion
   d. ecstasy

**20 eclogue**
   a. environmental study
   b. short poem
   c. position of the moon
   d. general discussion

ASSESS YOURSELF

**ASSESS YOURSELF** Ⓐ

# Playing the Detective

Your task here is to find the intruder among the following groups of words.

**1**
a. skivvy
b. servant
c. slave
d. factotum
e. employer

**2**
a. independence
b. freedom
c. coercion
d. liberty
e. licence

**3**
a. deviate
b. digress
c. branch out
d. decelerate
e. divaricate

**4**
a. initiate
b. procrastinate
c. delay
d. put off
e. postpone

**5**
a. vigilance
b. observation
c. watchfulness
d. inertia
e. invigilation

**6**
a. curiosity
b. zeal
c. nonchalance
d. officiousness
e. interest

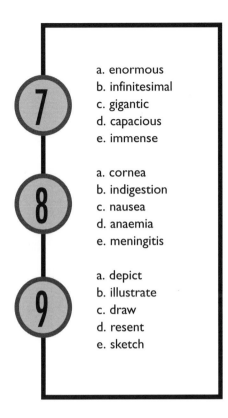

**7**
a. enormous
b. infinitesimal
c. gigantic
d. capacious
e. immense

**8**
a. cornea
b. indigestion
c. nausea
d. anaemia
e. meningitis

**9**
a. depict
b. illustrate
c. draw
d. resent
e. sketch

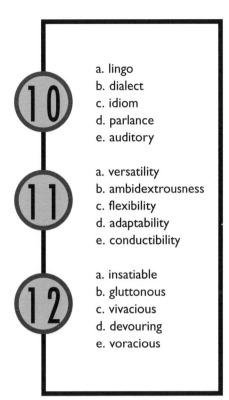

**10**
a. lingo
b. dialect
c. idiom
d. parlance
e. auditory

**11**
a. versatility
b. ambidextrousness
c. flexibility
d. adaptability
e. conductibility

**12**
a. insatiable
b. gluttonous
c. vivacious
d. devouring
e. voracious

# Speed Reading

Studies have shown that faster reading enhances learning and memory skills, as well as having the obvious benefit of saving time. Use the following passage to test your reading skills. All you need are a watch with a second hand to time yourself and a pen to record your starting and finishing times. Take care to read as you would normally – the aim here is to test your current ability, enabling you to determine how far you need to improve.

After timing your reading of the passage, tackle the multiple-choice comprehension test. Do this without referring to the passage at all, selecting the statement that most closely corresponds to the text.

**ASSESS YOURSELF**

ASSESS YOURSELF

# The Text

Eugène Boudin (1824-1898) is renowned for the many beach scenes he painted at Trouville, on the coast of Normandy in France. Coastal themes dominated his prolific output, which included almost 4,000 oil paintings. Having had a childhood strongly influenced by the sea, this lifelong artistic interest comes as little surprise.

He was born at Honfleur, a seaside town where Eugène's father Leonard had followed the tradition of countless Honfleur men before him by becoming a sailor. Leonard Boudin began his apprenticeship for the navy at the tender age of 11, later acting as a gunner in battles on the high seas against the English. He then swapped his bullets for a fishing rod, and began to earn a living fishing for cod. After eight years of marriage, Louis-Eugène was born on the 12th of July, 1824.

## Early Promise

Leonard Boudin's many years at sea enabled him to take charge of a small vessel trading between Rouen and Honfleur. His talented son was soon on board working as a cabin boy, and passed the time during breaks from his tasks by sketching. Even from a young age, Eugène Boudin was uplifted and inspired by life on the water.

Following a move to Le Havre in 1835, where his father took up a new shipping job, Eugène began to attend a school run by priests. Here, his artistic talents flourished. At the age of 12, however, this came to an abrupt end when Leonard decided to curtail his son's education and the boy began work as a printer's clerk in Le Havre. He then moved on to a job in a stationer's, where he worked his way up and became the owner's secretary. Despite offering little prospect of further promotion, Eugène received a gift from the owner of this stationer's that would have a vital influence on him: his first paintbox.

## A New Era Dawns

In 1838, the development of steamship traffic at this time enabled Leonard to find work on a steamer called *Le Français*, which frequented Honfleur and Le Havre. Eugène's mother also took to the seas, working as a stewardess on steamships in the area. Yet neither his parents' occupations, nor his early experience on the ocean, stimulated any desire in Eugène to follow a similar path. Instead, he formed a partnership with a foreman who had also worked for Lemasle, the stationers at which Eugène had previously been employed. This partnership gave birth to a new stationer's shop, and allowed Eugène to enjoy the work of visiting artists whose pictures they framed and displayed.

The personal contact that Boudin maintained with these artists and their work made him determined to become a painter himself. Despite words of warning offered by the artist Jean-François Millet about the precariousness of such a profession, Boudin carried on regardless. After arguing with his partner Jean Archer, in 1846, Boudin left their shop to embark on a life devoted to the art he loved. It was this powerful devotion alone that would keep him going through the difficult years that lay ahead.

# The Lure of the Sea

The hypnotic magic of the open water came to rule Boudin's otherwise miserable struggle to survive, and he often worked in the open air, overlooking the sea. Extremely modest sales of his work were enough to fuel his passion for painting, and his passion to learn more about the great masters.

Le Havre's offerings were limited – what Boudin needed to quench his thirst for knowledge was Paris, with its museums and stimulating artistic life. A year after ending his partnership, Boudin's scrimping and saving paid off and he arrived in Paris. What awaited him was not the land of his dreams – survival in the city was, in many ways, more of a struggle than the provincial life that he was accustomed to. Boudin did, however, spend endless hours studying the paintings he so revered, which taught him a great deal but also filled him with despair at what he saw as his own inadequacy. This despondency would remain with him throughout his artistic life.

Any travel was a large undertaking for a man so attached to his native land. Boudin's trip around Belgium and northern France was purely the result of a certain Baron Taylor, whose interest in art led him to run several societies that helped aspiring artists who needed financial support. This support helped all of the parties concerned: while Boudin toured around displaying his work, he sold lottery tickets in aid of artists in a similar situation to himself.

# Recognition at Last

Boudin continued to paint – seascapes, still lifes and copies of works by the great masters. His copies proved to be particularly profitable, largely due to commissions from Baron Taylor. His efforts were finally put on show properly for the first time in 1850, after his return to Le Havre. The exhibition enabled him to sell two of his paintings, bought by the purchasing committee of the art-loving society responsible for organizing the exhibition in the first place. It was from this society that Boudin received a grant of 3,600 francs, over three years. After remaining in Paris up to 1854, he was finally able to leave the confines of the capital to return to the pleasures of Le Havre, free to embark on his future career.

ASSESS YOURSELF

**ASSESS YOURSELF** (A)

# Comprehension

**1**
a. Boudin produced 4,000 pieces of work.
b. Boudin created just under 4,000 paintings on a coastal theme.
c. His total output included almost 4,000 oil paintings.

**2**
a. Before departing for Paris, Boudin enjoyed an extravagant lifestyle.
b. Boudin saved for a considerable time before leaving for Paris.
c. A grant funded Boudin's first trip to Paris.

**3**
a. Eugène Boudin's first job was at sea.
b. Eugène Boudin trained as a gunner.
c. Eugène Boudin started work when he was 12 years old.

**4**
a. Lemasle provided Eugène with his first set of paints.
b. Eugène's father was responsible for his first encounter with the world of painting.
c. Eugène was given his first box of paints while at a school run by priests.

**5**
a. Boudin's first exhibition took place in Paris.
b. The first significant exhibition of Boudin's paintings was in Le Havre.
c. Boudin never had a proper display of his work.

**6**
a. Leonard Boudin worked on the first steamship.
b. Leonard Boudin found work during the rise in the use of steamships.
c. Leonard Boudin helped develop the use of steamships.

**7**
a. Eugène was always confident about his work.
b. Eugène continually criticized his own work.
c. Eugène became known as an art critic.

**8**
a. Much of Eugène's work stemmed from his study of the sea.
b. As a young man, Eugène dreamed of a career on the waves.
c. Eugène preferred to work indoors.

**9**
a. Baron Taylor purchased Eugène's early still lifes.
b. Eugène's three-year stay in Paris was financed by Baron Taylor.
c. Eugène was commissioned by the Baron to make copies of works by the great masters.

**10**
a. Eugène's father emulated many previous Honfleur seamen.
b. Eugène was born in Le Havre.
c. Eugène was born in Trouville.

An estimated 40% of adults across the world are said to be unable to read. Reading is not just a question of making a concentrated effort to recognize a series of visual symbols. It also becomes an integral part of the way we process information, enabling us to read words quicker than we could say them – we've all had the experience of the eyes being swifter than the tongue.

# In Control

In general terms, the processing of language is controlled by the left half of the brain. Within this half, specific regions are responsible for different types of language manipulation. Being able to write, and the ability to control your voice, stems from processes that take place in the frontal lobe. Damage to the parietal lobe, toward the back of the brain, can result in alexia, a condition where it becomes difficult to read words without confusing the letters. The temporal lobe, located by the ear, and the outer layer of the parietal lobe, control the capacity to understand what it being said to us. Harming these areas can result in deafness – if this happens to a child, learning to read can be an upward struggle.

# The Process of Reading

We all appreciate that efficient reading skills can extend our understanding and vocabulary, while a poor reading technique and selection of reading matter can substantially hinder our progress. Focusing exclusively on reading as rapidly as possible often results in a failure to grasp the meaning of the material, and the reader may need to begin all over again. The ideal reading technique involves the use of careful, considered skimming strategies. For example, an initial scan of a piece of text gives the reader a broad overview, enabling the brain to focus properly on the general subject matter. Just as the body needs warming up before vigorous exercise, so too does the mind.

PUT IT IN PERSPECTIVE

# The Eyes Have It

Different reading techniques are often linked to eye movement. Studies have shown how reading requires a continual, rapid cycle of stops and starts, the eyes focusing suddenly on a batch of letters before swooping on to the next batch. Due to the brain's preference for chunks of information, as opposed to single bits, the more words that can be absorbed at a glance, the easier and quicker it is to learn.

The overview obtained by effective skimming can make a huge difference to your powers of comprehension and recall. There is no specific scanning method – the eyes may wander vertically, horizontally and diagonally across the page, focusing on individual key words, phrases and titles. A page may be scanned in anything from 2 to 20 seconds. The speed and technique is unique to each individual, as are the resulting benefits.

Perhaps most importantly, skimming can lessen the fear that many people feel when reading something new. Escaping the feeling that you must concentrate equally on every word helps to set the mind at ease. The more relaxed reading that will follow on from this makes the entire process altogether more rewarding.

# Flexibility is the Key

Whatever your reading speed, a good reader needs to maintain a flexible approach. Obviously, a complicated passage requires greater study, with slower reading and less text skimmed or skipped. It has been shown that fast readers may study at a pace similar to slower workers in such sections, but more efficient reading and scanning of less important passages enables their overall speed to be maintained.

The major key to efficient retention and recall of written information is understanding, not merely being able to repeat something "parrot-fashion." If you have a high level of understanding, the brain stays sharply focused on the subject matter and you will find it far easier to read quickly. The foundation stones of effective understanding and efficient reading technique are:

- The ability to relate individual words and sentences to the context as a whole

- Maintaining and focusing your interest by taking breaks, making notes, perhaps referring to other texts, making more heavy-going material accessible by linking it with other subjects that you enjoy more

- Keeping fresh by pausing every so often

Reading can provide us with a whole world of fascinating education and enjoyment – but only if you learn to read actively, with a questioning mind, using it as a springboard for finding out even more.

There are all kinds of easy ways in which you can improve your reading skills.

# Making the Most of Your Daily Read

Newspapers provide an invaluable source of reading material, often helping us to improve both our vocabulary range and our speed reading skills. Delving into a range of different newspapers can make us more aware of the different styles of language that are effective in different situations, as well as providing interest and variety. Scanning through a paper helps you to locate articles of immediate interest, improving your ability to focus on what is strictly relevant, and discarding what isn't.

## Increasing Your Speeds

Now that you have a general notion of your reading speed, you can formulate a plan of self-improvement. For example, try selecting an article of approximately 1,000 words. Time how long it takes you to read this, and then write a brief summary of the piece to test your overall comprehension. Try to assess yourself as honestly as possible, or you will gain little from the exercise. Find your reading speed per minute by following the process explained on page 43: count the number of words in the article, multiply it by 60, and divide this by your time in seconds. A reasonable amount of practice should result in an increased speed of around 100.

## Test Your Scanning Abilities

The exercise overleaf is designed to test your ability to scan a page for the most important information, giving you greater understanding and improved reading efficiency. Your task is to work through each line, glancing at the first group of letters, then marking the position of its twin, positioned somewhere else in each line. As you work through, the letter groups get larger. A metronome may help you to maintain speed – set the pace to correspond with the time it takes you to get through one of the first lines. Trying to stick to this rhythm as you progress will help you to broaden the range of characters your eyes can take in within a given time.

| | | | | | | | |
|---|---|---|---|---|---|---|---|
| BA | GU | B C | ST | IN | LK | BA | AA |
| OJ | LP | TG | BC | SE | OJ | QJ | BR |
| CT | IP | CT | EY | KB | FG | TH | NO |
| LF | YU | BU | LF | UB | DY | IH | BK |
| VT | VT | KI | CT | IU | PV | EJ | OG |
| UI | HD | TB | LK | OG | CR | UM | UI |
| DE | YU | JU | KI | DE | SG | KU | OL |
| MO | DT | MO | RT | UH | MV | DE | YG |
| CX | TE | JH | JI | CX | KT | CT | EC |
| OT | GY | UI | BF | TD | OT | NU | OP |
| CV | GT | CV | JY | IJ | OM | LP | DW |
| KP | HU | TE | PK | KP | RT | VD | IN |
| CT | ES | WI | UN | HO | PL | BC | CT |
| BY | UI | JN | BY | ER | OJ | LN | CT |
| VY | IO | FT | PO | JH | CT | WS | VY |
| UO | TF | ER | VT | DY | UO | KH | DT |
| PO | PN | UT | FY | IN | PO | HY | ER |
| NU | TY | MI | OP | MV | FT | ED | NU |
| BU | TI | OP | MI | YU | BU | DT | BY |
| VY | ER | VY | UO | JO | PL | MU | YU |

| | | | | | | | |
|---|---|---|---|---|---|---|---|
| BYT | CRU | OPK | BNT | UIO | TYD | BYT | UIM |
| VHI | FTY | VSR | EDI | KOM | VHI | DTW | QAU |
| MOL | BYR | MOL | PHI | TBD | YUI | NOF | GHI |
| WXT | GUE | WAI | HUB | WXT | UBI | MOP | HIM |
| EUT | IUY | EUT | GON | BIE | EUF | YBI | UIO |
| BJD | YRU | DFG | IOU | NUI | VHT | DRT | BJD |
| LPB | UTD | CTS | HIM | LPB | CTE | UGM | NIT |
| NIB | HUI | DTE | CUG | NIB | PKT | DEA | JIB |
| YTE | MIT | UI | HFR | YTE | CFT | LOP | YUI |
| VTY | UIO | VTY | RSE | YTU | HJI | NPO | MIG |
| CTY | UIO | JNR | ERT | VJU | CSE | RTF | CTY |
| IOH | CTE | UIV | SJW | TFA | IOH | OPB | CRA |
| GYM | KOI | VZE | GYM | VUS | WQA | VRI | OPL |
| NID | RYG | NIA | WQE | RCG | IOM | NID | PLF |
| VUE | KOP | LFE | ZPO | VUE | ASU | REL | BUI |
| NZE | RTY | IGS | BOP | LMV | STQ | UOI | NZE |
| QRT | UYF | BHU | PAS | LGR | WQD | QRT | UIV |
| BDT | GUA | BDT | OPG | UTW | DFC | BZH | JUO |
| CAR | CAR | TYU | CGQ | IGS | PLN | ETU | CAT |
| MKE | UTV | HSM | MKI | VHA | TEC | MKE | IUB |

| | | | | | | | |
|---|---|---|---|---|---|---|---|
| MAOW | VYSE | YYJV | MAOW | UYRV | MOPD | GTEH | NIPL |
| BIDT | FTEY | NUIO | MODE | UYIB | BIDT | YUIN | MPLY |
| SDWR | YUIO | JCEN | NJOM | NSTR | KOPB | MODT | SDWR |
| MPLD | UITB | XDRW | YUIB | MKOR | YUIJ | MPLD | REWY |
| CSTW | ITHB | VGIR | CSTW | HJIM | MPLH | UIOD | ETUB |
| NUOM | JHGD | RYUV | NUIE | NUOM | KPLG | TYIC | EYYC |
| BUET | HUIP | BUET | DEAU | IJFO | MIFT | ECSU | INFT |
| MPLG | YRWE | BHIP | MOPD | RTUO | MPLG | YUID | RTUV |
| BUTE | IOHN | TETY | BUTE | TYIF | JKKR | RTUV | NOIY |
| VDTE | TYUB | NIOF | TYIU | NOPF | VDTE | TYIB | MIOO |
| NDAN | RTIJ | BHIL | PFTW | RUVJ | NDAN | KOPL | NCTT |
| OPLM | TPKG | AHUI | OPLM | VTSR | TYUO | MOJU | FTUO |
| BHDQ | YIIB | GIUM | VYUO | BUSE | YUON | BHDQ | OKMG |
| PCZE | TUOB | CJOR | OMVB | TDEY | PCZE | IONF | WRUJ |
| FALK | IOGD | GTAF | UFAK | LUIU | FALK | OPHC | EOHF |
| VHIF | GYTI | BHRE | OIHF | JTEF | LKUH | VHIF | IOKH |
| HDEI | OPKV | DSHE | TUIB | HDEI | OPLM | VSIH | KYVL |
| UPAI | UPAI | MKOF | EROB | CTSR | YIOJ | BAGU | OMAK |
| LJST | YIHB | LJST | HUOO | NCTW | TYIB | MKSY | OPNC |
| BAJI | YUOK | BGST | UPKN | BAJI | PLBD | TUOB | GHAJ |

| | | | | | | | |
|---|---|---|---|---|---|---|---|
| CEWIQ | OPKLC | CEWIQ | LNVK | STUMD | VUSWD | TRUGF | BIDMF |
| MSIFO | VGJOD | JBHUS | TYUKH | GHHTR | MSIFO | FGHJT | DRFUI |
| AVGHJ | TINBM | FTUUY | GHUIO | AVGHJ | OPOLM | GYUIU | VTYEJ |
| BUDTE | BHILJ | VBHYR | HIUJN | KLIPO | VHGUR | HJIOM | BUDTE |
| VHUIO | KOOPJ | DFTTR | NKOLK | VHUIO | PLVGY | RTJIO | CGHJK |
| ADFTT | UOIJK | MLKOI | ADFTT | UOINV | GYIOK | BHJTR | IOONF |
| KGUYR | HGUIM | GHJUY | TYTFJ | IOIHH | RTUYB | KGUYR | BVHUT |
| FAJDE | TYIKM | VHJKM | RTIOC | FAJDE | YIUON | FKJYM | FHTHM |
| LVGSD | YUIHV | KIOUI | FTIUB | LPFES | LVGSD | YIOKG | RTIJF |
| AMOPH | GHUII | NJAIU | YUIOK | AMOPH | DRQWT | PIREV | NJIUT |
| SGUAI | YGERI | OPJHF | SGUAI | PLMGR | UIOMF | BTGYO | BHTJM |
| NAGSH | KOLIU | HJSKA | HJIUY | IOIMN | NAGSH | UOJMN | GHJAY |
| LSNXH | YUIOS | BNJSY | KYIAO | BHJSU | LSNXH | UIAOM | SGETQ |
| ANSHR | TYAIO | NBSFT | TAIJN | ANSHR | UIOSK | BBBSG | JAJYS |
| OITFS | HTYEW | RYUOA | OGABS | HSYRS | OITFS | NHGSK | OPPAN |
| ERLAE | HSOAM | HGSYK | ERLAE | JOPMF | PAFST | YUIOS | BAHJO |
| SJDHF | SJDHF | UIOPK | SKYRE | JIOMG | FAVHJ | KLPO0 | BFSTY |
| LANSH | JIOIT | GTYJN | KOOGR | LANSH | UIOPK | BFRTY | NGHOK |
| IWTQY | MAHST | JHQHG | IWTQY | IOISH | NMAJS | NNSJS | USIOA |
| JSHWW | JSHWW | YYIOP | JLFSW | QDTUO | NFSTT | YUIOK | GSFSK |

You can devise similar tests yourself, using letters, numbers or other symbols. Alternatively, try skimming text for a particular (common) word. A conscious effort to read faster and skim better will inevitably improve your skills without a huge amount of effort.

TEST IT OUT

# Stretch Your Wordpower

To extend your vocabulary, you will find numerous written tests similar to those in the self-assessment section in other books of this nature. However, the general context of the word is often missing in such tests. Wider reading of a challenging nature, exploiting the full range of books, magazines and newspapers, will help you to develop a more accurate and varied vocabulary.

When writing, having a thesaurus and dictionary to hand provides instant access to a language goldmine. Spelling difficulties can be lessened by examining the word visually – letting your mind absorb the shape, size and quantity of letters. Play around with the word mentally, creating its own identity in your mind. Stimulating the mind in these ways will also help to unlock all kinds of words that you had forgotten you even knew!

Knowledge of some common Latin, Greek and English prefixes and suffixes is always helpful when you don't have a dictionary to hand, because it allows you to make informed guesses about word meanings. A brief list follows.

| PREFIX STEM AND EXAMPLE | DEFINITION OF PREFIX | SUFFIX STEM AND EXAMPLE | DEFINITION OF SUFFIX |
|---|---|---|---|
| ab-stract | away from | enjoy-able | capable of |
| ad-jacent | next to/towards | cardi-ac | pertaining to |
| an-aphrodisiac | not/without | advant-age | action/locality |
| ante-date | before | annu-al | pertaining to |
| anti-freeze | opposing/against | abund-ance | state/action |
| arch-angel | principal | pleas-ant | causing/performing action |
| auto-biography | self | secret-ary | dealing with/ |
| bene-volent | well | | place for |
| bi-focal | twice | anim-ate | cause to be |
| bio-logy | life | arti-cle | indicating smallness |
| cent-enary | one hundred | wis-dom | power/condition |
| centi-grade | one hundreth | wax-en | made of |
| circum-ference | around | kitt-en | small |
| com-pose | together/with | acqu-eous | pertaining to |
| con-tain | together/with | sing-er | belonging to |
| contra-vene | against | conval-escent | steadily becoming |
| de-compose | reversal | coni-ferous | bearing |
| demi-god | half | fanci-ful | full of |
| dia-meter | through/during | beauti-fy | to make |
| dis-like | reversal | widow-hood | state/condition |
| ex-hale | out of | rept-ile | capable of being |
| extra-sensory | outside/beyond | redd-ish | relationship/similarity |
| fore-see | before | | |

| PREFIX STEM AND EXAMPLE | DEFINITION OF PREFIX | SUFFIX STEM AND EXAMPLE | DEFINITION OF SUFFIX |
|---|---|---|---|
| <u>hemi</u>-sphere | half | skeptic-<u>ism</u> | state/system |
| <u>homo</u>-logous | same | pharmac-<u>ist</u> | one who does |
| <u>inter</u>-act | between | hepat-<u>itis</u> | medical: inflammation |
| <u>intro</u>-spection | inside/into | capabil-<u>ity</u> | state/quality |
| <u>mal</u>-evolent | bad | civil-<u>ize</u> | to make/act |
| <u>mega</u>-lopolis | great | gut-<u>less</u> | free from/lacking |
| <u>micro</u>-dot | small | socio-<u>logy</u> | doctrine/knowledge |
| <u>mis</u>-fit | wrongly | amuse-<u>ment</u> | state/act of |
| <u>mono</u>-logue | single/one | thermo-<u>meter</u> | measure of |
| <u>non</u>-sense | not | matri-<u>mony</u> | condition |
| <u>ob</u>-struct | in the way | vigil-<u>ance</u> | state/condition |
| <u>para</u>-graph | beside/near | vigil-<u>ancy</u> | state/quality |
| <u>per</u>-forate | through | cub-<u>oid</u> | resembling |
| <u>peri</u>-meter | around/about | conduct-<u>or</u> | one who |
| <u>poly</u>-gon | many/much | | /thing which |
| <u>post</u>-orbital | after | verb-<u>ose</u> | full of |
| <u>pre</u>-eminant | before | garrul-<u>ous</u> | full of |
| <u>pro</u>-vide | before/in front | tele-<u>scope</u> | aid to sight |
| <u>pseudo</u>-nym | false | censor-<u>ship</u> | state/office of |
| <u>retro</u>-active | back/backwards | trouble-<u>some</u> | full of/like |
| <u>semi</u>-breve | half | young-<u>ster</u> | one who |
| <u>sub</u>-editor | under/beneath | | /association |
| <u>super</u>-sonic | above/over | fanta-<u>sy</u> | state |
| <u>syn</u>-thesis | with/together | percep-<u>tion</u> | abtract state |
| <u>tele</u>-cast | distant/far | apti-<u>tude</u> | state/degree of |
| <u>trans</u>-atlantic | across/beyond | glob-<u>ule</u> | small |
| <u>ultra</u>-marine | beyond | back-<u>ward</u> | direction |
| <u>uni</u>-lateral | one | clock-<u>wise</u> | direction/manner |
| <u>vice</u>-president | in place of | murk-<u>y</u> | condition |

Setting attainable goals over a regular course of reading should encourage you to practice and lead to great improvement. Challenge your mind constantly – it needs to be well-nourished, and not simply fed on junk food.

TEST IT OUT

**TEST IT OUT**

## Test Your Wordpower

**Answers**

1.c  2.b  3.a  4.a  5.c  6.d  7.a  8.b  9.a  10.d
11.b  12.b  13.c  14.c  15.b  16.a  17.d  18.b  19.a  20.b

**Your Score**

0-5: Poor. You've probably just got a little lazy over the years – make improving your vocabulary a priority now and you'll soon see what a difference it can make.

6-10: Average. You, too, will benefit from broader knowledge.

11-15: Very good. But keep trying even harder.

16-20: Excellent.

## Playing the Detective

**Answers**

1.e  2.c  3.d  4.a  5.d  6.c
7.b  8.a  9.d  10.e  11.e  12.c

**Your Score**

Below 6   Poor. But that just means plenty of room for improvement.

7 or 8    Average. Quite acceptable range – keep working on it.

9 or 10   Pretty good. You have a wide vocabulary at your disposal.

11 or 12 Excellent. Although you can never know enough where words are concerned.

## Speed Reading

**Comprehension:**
**Answers**

1.c  2.b  3.a  4.a  5.b
6.b  7.b  8.a  9.c  10.a

**Your Score**

Under 7 statements correct: You are perhaps not concentrating as well as you could, or are simply reading too quickly.

7 or more correct: You have a fairly satisfactory level of comprehension – but it could always be better!

**To calculate your reading speed:**

1. Multiply the number of words in the passage by the number of seconds in a minute, which in this case would be 50,400 (840 x 60).

2. Divide 50,400 by the total number of seconds it took you to read the passage.

So, with a total reading time of 206 seconds, your reading speed would be 245 words per minute.

**Your Score**

245 words per minute is a fairly average score. A score of around 200 could certainly do with a bit of work, while one of 600 is pretty exceptional.

# Understanding Numbers

The following tests give you the opportunity to assess your numerical skills using the four basic mathematical operations – addition, subtraction, multiplication and division. You have up to 90 minutes to work through the questions. After assessing your skills, read on to discover how to make the numbers in your life work for you.

**1.** Replace the question marks to make the string of calculations complete.

| 27 | + | ? | = | 71 |
|---|---|---|---|---|
|  |  |  |  | × |

| 84 | - | ? | = | 55 | 3 |
|---|---|---|---|---|---|
| = |  |  |  | + | = |
| ? |  | 124 | = | ? | ? |
| × |  |  |  |  | - |
| 12 | = | ? | ÷ | ? | = | 69 |

**2.** During a day out shopping for a forthcoming business trip, Sandra bought 12 boxes of Belgian chocolates, priced at $7 each, for which she handed over a money order already made out for $100. She then added the change to the sum of 7 $50 bills and 7 loose dollar bills she had in her wallet. After buying 4 tickets to a show, costing $33 each, how much money did Sandra have left over?

**ASSESS YOURSELF**

**ASSESS YOURSELF** Ⓐ

**3.** Study the triangles to find the recurring pattern that will enable you to replace the letters with the correct figures.

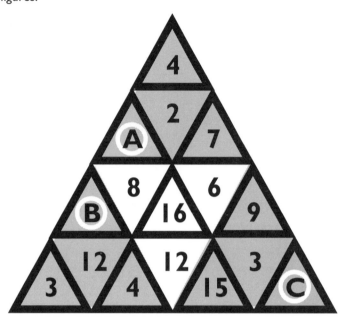

**4.** If:
A is a third of B
A = 3C − 4
B = 8 + 5C
then what value does C have?

**5.** How many seconds will it take for 7 dogs to eat 49 biscuits if they each eat one every 5 seconds?

**6.** What number comes next in each of the sequences below?

    **a)** 160, 40, 10, ?

    **b)** 7, 22, 67, ?

    **c)** 68, 36, 20, 12, ?

    **d)** 145, 134, 122, 109, ?

    **e)** 33, 24, 34, 23, ?

**7.** What number replaces the question mark below the grid?

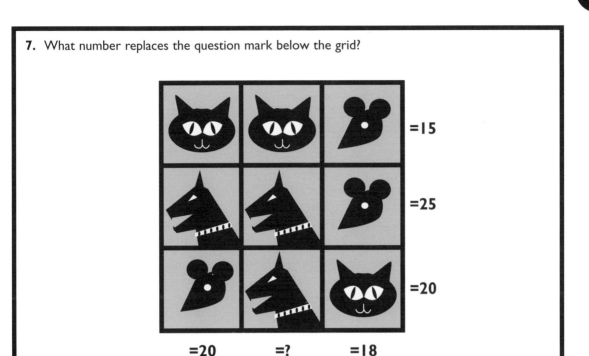

=15
=25
=20

=20    =?    =18

**8.** How far does the Adams family have to travel to visit their relations if they drive at 60 mph for 20 minutes, spend 3½ hours at a constant 75 mph, and drive for the last 25 minutes at a speed of 40 mph, during which time they stop for 2 minutes to seek directions?

**9.** Convert each of the following series of numbers into a correct mathematical equation; each time, using 2 or 3 of the basic mathematical operations. You may group the numbers as you wish.

    **a)** 2 2 2 2 2 = 66

    **b)** 4 4 4 4 4 = 55

    **c)** 7 7 7 7 7 = 22

    **d)** 6 6 6 6 6 = 11

    **e)** 3 3 3 3 3 = 66

**10.** If P is half of Q when Q equals the square root of 3 dozen, then what is the numerical value of P?

**11.** At a birthday party, each child is given some chocolates. There are 6 five-year-olds, 6 six-year-olds and 6 seven-year-olds present. If each child receives 3 times as many chocolates as their age in years, how many chocolates are handed out altogether?

**ASSESS YOURSELF**

**ASSESS YOURSELF** A

**12.** Which symbol would balance the third scale?

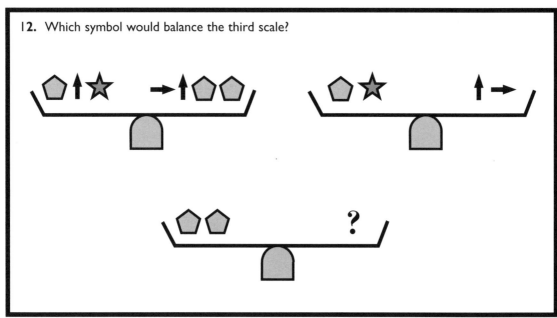

**13.** If Z is the square of 8, what is X if X is 3 times the value of Y, which is a quarter of Z?

**14.** On average, 5% of pupils at a particular school are absent each day. With 3 classes of 24, 4 classes of 27 and 5 classes of 32, how many children are expected to attend each day?

**15.** A clock correctly reads 9:30 on one particular Saturday morning, but then starts to run too fast, gaining 4 minutes each hour. What is the actual time when the clock displays 5 p.m.?

**16.** Study the 3 pyramids to discover the correct numerical value of each question mark.

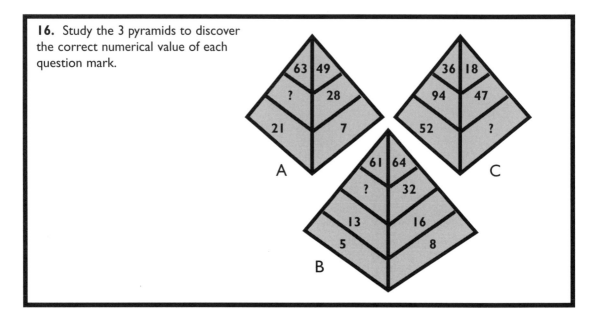

**17.** Janine invests $200 on January 1st each year in a savings account for her granddaughter. Annual interest of 10% is earned on all the money, payable on December 31st. How much money is in the account on January 2nd in the third year of the account?

**18.** How much is M worth if 8M − 3N = 29 and 5N − 13 = 32?

**19.** A desk-making workshop is held one weekend, and various teams from the north and south of the area are taking part. Glue is needed to make these desks. If 60% of the 15 northern teams and 55% of the 20 southern teams managed to obtain it, how many teams are left without glue?

**20.** According to the other 2 pictures, how many birds do the 3 clouds lack?

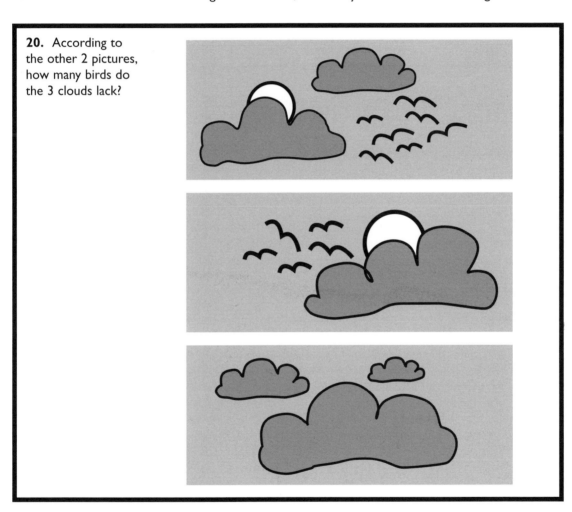

**21.** What do S and T equal if 4R = 6S = 8T and 7R = 42?

**22.** A cube-shaped swimming pool is drained to change the water. The water had a depth of exactly 5 feet. How long will it take to empty the pool if the water level decreases by 3 inches every 4 minutes?

> **Multiplication is vexation, Division is as bad; The rule of three doth puzzle me, And practice drives me mad.**
>
> (Anon.)

If the prospect of confronting a page crammed with figures makes you shudder, you are not alone. Numbers can fill the most literate and educated of people with fear, but you will soon discover that most of these fears are groundless.

After working through the self-assessment section, you may already have realized that most of the tests are much simpler than they first appeared. Consider the shopping problem. Delete all the extraneous text and you are left with a few basic figures from which a simple series of calculations lead you to the answer.

The most important things to remember when dealing with numbers are:

● Don't panic

● Keep things simple

Whether attempting problems like the ones included here, or sifting through mounds of paperwork to work out your disposable income, keep the data as simple and well organized as possible.

# Building Barriers

We are bombarded with numbers in one form or another from a very young age. As children, we can easily work out that one of the 6 parts of a certain game is missing or that our pocket money is short by a certain amount. We happily count up to large numbers during a game of hide-and-seek. Yet as soon as numbers are connected with school and work, our previously casual attitude is often transformed.

Once we are criticized for a careless mathematical error, the fear of making further mistakes often causes us to build a complete mental barricade where any numbers are concerned. Such fear inevitably prevents progress, encouraging a loathing for the subject, and a refusal to learn.

The power of your brain cannot be underestimated. You may wonder at the sophistication and speed with which today's computers hurry through complicated calculations, but creating a computer with the abilities of the human mind would be impossible. The size of such a machine would be unmanageable – as would the instruction manual! So have confidence in yourself next time you are faced with pages of calculations. Don't always reach for a calculator – take the opportunity to make your mind work harder, and the practice will soon start to make a difference.

# Making Numbers Work for You

Despite the "vexation" that mathematics may provoke, it is actually a simplification of everyday life. Numbers often act as a straightforward code for much more complex ideas, so the notion that you can't tackle them at all would seem to be completely illogical. How often have you switched on the news to hear a lengthy description of a company's performance that could have been represented far more succinctly by a graph? Of course numbers and statistics can always be manipulated and used to impress – mainly because most people are too afraid of figures to question them. So don't believe another person's calculations as a matter of course – be on your guard!

From building the Great Pyramids to the latest advances in computer technology, mathematics has always played an important part of human life. Each advance has the potential to bring further benefit, so concentrate on making numbers work for you, and don't simply shy away from them.

**PUT IT IN PERSPECTIVE**

PUT IT IN PERSPECTIVE

# TEST IT OUT

To do or not to do – that is the question. It is impossible to master any level of mathematics by just reading about it. Being confident with numbers requires practice and experimentation. If the very idea makes you nervous, don't automatically reject it before giving it a go. A little practice can rapidly lead to heartening results. As with any game, you have to learn the rules before you start to play.

The number tips that follow are designed simply as an aid to basic numeracy – it's up to you to decide how far you need to take it.

# Multiplication and Division

Does the mere mention of "multiplication tables" bring back some of your least cherished childhood memories, of schooldays filled with endless repetition and tests? If so, don't despair. Multiplication is very useful in everyday life, as you find when you need to work out how much 6 boxes of chocolates at $7 each will cost during a Christmas shopping spree. Chances are, you will tackle the necessary calculations very effectively, because there is no teacher peering over your desk, pressurizing you for an answer; no one ready to laugh at your mistakes. If you take your time, and make a point of working things out in your head, rapid multiplication could soon become second nature.

For simple calculations, a multiplication and division table is provided below for your reference. To multiply two numbers together, go down the column of one until you meet the row of the other to arrive at the answer. So, 6 lots of $7 costs $42. For division, go down the column headed with the smaller number until you find the larger number that is to be divided into. The row number gives the answer. So, if you have 72 inches of timber that you want to divide into 8-inch lengths, working down column 8 until you reach 72 shows that you will have 9 lengths altogether. But if you have 90 inches and still want 8-inch lengths, find the number closest to 90 in column 8 (which is 88) to discover that you can cut 11 complete lengths with 2 inches of timber left over.

**COLUMN**

| ROW | 2 | 3 | 4 | 5 | 6 | 7 | 8 | 9 | 10 | 11 | 12 | 13 | 14 | 15 |
|---|---|---|---|---|---|---|---|---|---|---|---|---|---|---|
| 2 | 4 | 6 | 8 | 10 | 12 | 14 | 16 | 18 | 20 | 22 | 24 | 26 | 28 | 30 |
| 3 | 6 | 9 | 12 | 15 | 18 | 21 | 24 | 27 | 30 | 33 | 36 | 39 | 42 | 45 |
| 4 | 8 | 12 | 16 | 20 | 24 | 28 | 32 | 36 | 40 | 44 | 48 | 52 | 56 | 60 |
| 5 | 10 | 15 | 20 | 25 | 30 | 35 | 40 | 45 | 50 | 55 | 60 | 65 | 70 | 75 |
| 6 | 12 | 18 | 24 | 30 | 36 | 42 | 48 | 54 | 60 | 66 | 72 | 78 | 84 | 90 |
| 7 | 14 | 21 | 28 | 35 | 42 | 49 | 56 | 63 | 70 | 77 | 84 | 91 | 98 | 105 |
| 8 | 16 | 24 | 32 | 40 | 48 | 56 | 64 | 72 | 80 | 88 | 96 | 104 | 112 | 120 |
| 9 | 18 | 27 | 36 | 45 | 54 | 63 | 72 | 81 | 90 | 99 | 108 | 117 | 126 | 135 |
| 10 | 20 | 30 | 40 | 50 | 60 | 70 | 80 | 90 | 100 | 110 | 120 | 130 | 140 | 150 |
| 11 | 22 | 33 | 44 | 55 | 66 | 77 | 88 | 99 | 110 | 121 | 132 | 143 | 154 | 165 |
| 12 | 24 | 36 | 48 | 60 | 72 | 84 | 96 | 108 | 120 | 132 | 144 | 156 | 168 | 180 |
| 13 | 26 | 39 | 52 | 65 | 78 | 91 | 104 | 117 | 130 | 143 | 156 | 169 | 182 | 195 |
| 14 | 28 | 42 | 56 | 70 | 84 | 98 | 112 | 126 | 140 | 154 | 168 | 182 | 196 | 210 |
| 15 | 30 | 45 | 60 | 75 | 90 | 105 | 120 | 135 | 150 | 165 | 180 | 195 | 210 | 225 |

Sometimes problems can actually be solved more quickly without the use of a table, or even a calculator. This is especially true when dealing with the numbers 5 and 10. For example, if you want to buy 10 notebooks priced at $4.50 each, you will be spending $45:

$$4.5 \times 10 = 45$$

To multiply a decimal number by 10, all you have to do is move the decimal point one place to the right. If you are working with a whole number, all you have to do is add a nought: 10 boxes each containing 12 pens hold 120 pens in total.

It therefore follows that, to divide by 10, you remove a nought (if there is one) or shift a decimal point one place to the left. Where a whole number such as 45 is concerned, it is sometimes easier to view it as 45.0, so that the position of the decimal point is clear in your mind.

When dealing with the number 5, remind yourself that it is simply half of 10. So, if you are multiplying by 5, add a nought to the relevant number, or shift the decimal point to the right, and then divide by 2. Five of the notebooks priced at $4.50 cost $22.50:

$$4.5 \times 10 = 45$$
$$45 \div 2 = 22.5$$

To divide the 120 pens between 5 people is just a case of common sense – doubling 120 and dividing that by 10. Knowing how to multiply a number by 10 gives you enough information to deal with both multiplication and division involving the numbers 5, 10, and other related numbers, too. Some of these are summarized below. For division, follow the same process but in reverse.

| TO MULTIPLY BY: | ADD THIS MANY NOUGHTS: | AND DIVIDE BY: (MULTIPLY BY) |
|:---:|:---:|:---:|
| 5 | 1 | 2 |
| 10 | 1 | 1 |
| 20 | 1 | (2) |
| 25 | 2 | 4 |
| 100 | 2 | 1 |
| 1000 | 3 | 1 |

# Getting to Grips With Fractions

Whether dividing a cake into equal portions, or understanding statistics in a newspaper report, you probably have to deal with fractions every day, although you may not be aware of it. They are easy to cope with as long as you know the logical rules.

## Multiplication

Can you remember the rule for multiplying fractions from your schooldays? Even if you can't, the chances are that you know how to do this instinctively. If you had to divide a cake into 2, you would cut it in half; if you had to share that cake between 4 people, you would cut it into quarters. So you obviously know that half of a half is a quarter. Expressed mathematically:

$$\frac{1}{2} \times \frac{1}{2} = \frac{1}{4}$$

This is simply a case of multiplying the numbers above the line (the numerators) together, and the numbers below the line (the denominators) together. This rule applies to any fractions:

$$\frac{2}{3} \times \frac{3}{4} = \frac{6}{12}$$

In this case, for example, 2 out of 3 friends are sharing the remaining three quarters of a cake.

However, the fraction $\frac{6}{12}$ can easily be simplified. When both the numbers above and below the line can be divided exactly by the same whole number, that number can be deleted, or cancelled out. This is because multiplying both parts of the fraction by the same number does not alter the value of the fraction. So:

$$\frac{6}{12} = \frac{6 \times 1}{6 \times 2} = \frac{1}{2}$$

# Division

Dividing one fraction by another is made easy by simply knowing one useful trick. Just swap one fraction's components around, and multiply by the other. Say you have 2 cakes, each of a different size. One cake fits 1½ times into 3/4 of another:

$$\frac{3}{4} \div \frac{1}{2} = \frac{3}{4} \times \frac{2}{1} = \frac{6}{4} = 1\frac{1}{2}$$

# Addition and Subtraction

If you want to add 2 fractions, and both have the same number below the line, get your answer by simply adding together the 2 numbers above the line. This is totally logical when you consider that combining the 2 halves of a broken plate makes 1 whole plate. This would be expressed mathematically as:

$$\frac{1}{2} + \frac{1}{2} = \frac{1+1}{2} = 1 \text{ and } \underline{\text{not}} \frac{1+1}{2+2} \text{ which equals } \frac{2}{4} \text{ or } \frac{1}{2}$$

As already shown, multiplying both parts of a fraction by the same number does not affect its value. So to make the numbers below the line on both fractions the same, multiply both parts of one fraction by the number below the line, or denominator, of the other. This may sound confusing, but when expressed mathematically, the process should become much clearer:

$$\frac{1}{2} + \frac{3}{4} = \frac{4 \times 1}{4 \times 2} + \frac{3 \times 2}{4 \times 2} = \frac{4+6}{4 \times 2} = \frac{10}{8} = 1\frac{2}{8} = 1\frac{1}{4}$$

Once you have overcome any needless fear of fractions, you can see from the examples above that they can greatly simplify what would otherwise be extremely complex problems if, for example, they were expressed entirely in words.

TEST IT OUT

**TEST IT OUT** T

# What's the Point of Percentages?

Fractions can easily be expressed as percentages. A percentage is a proportion of a whole, and that whole is 100 – "per" means "for" and "cent" means 100. We are continually bombarded with percentages: 25% reduction on sale goods; 67% examination pass rate; 8% of a town's population unemployed. Because they sound so important, many people are intimidated by them, but they are really just a way of measuring information so that you can get an accurate picture.

In order to convert a fraction into a percentage, just multiply it by 100. So, if 3/4 of those attending your evening class passed the French exam, you know that:

$$\frac{3}{4} \times 100 = \frac{300}{4}$$

This means that 75% of the students passed, or 3 out of every 4 people. So logically, dividing a percentage by 100 produces the corresponding fraction:

$$75\% = \frac{75}{100} = \frac{3}{4}$$

When calculations involve percentages, it is essential that these are converted into fractions rather than just omitting the percentage symbol. Otherwise, you may get rather more than you bargained for!

## Discounts

You will often come across percentages when dealing with special offers on goods. When you want to work out how much you save by buying a washing machine priced at $450 that is reduced in price by 12%, all you have to do is:
divide the original price by 100, and then multiply by the percentage in question, or
12 x $4.50 = $54

To find the price you will pay, simply take $54 away from the original price to give $396.

If you just want to find the final price, you can divide the original price by 100, and multiply that by 100 minus the discount offered: **100 – 12 = 88%**
An easy tip to remember every time you have to deal with fractions or percentages is that "of" in this context means "multiply".
So 88% of 200 is

$$\frac{88}{100} \times 200 = 176$$

# Price Plus Percentage

To calculate a price that needs to include an additional percentage, for example if you had to add a tax of 20% onto the price of goods, follow this routine:
Calculate the 20% as before, and then add it to the original price. If you have a calculator handy, or you want a bit of a challenge, then the original price can be multiplied by 1 plus the percentage divided by 100.

So, the final cost of a tool costing $80 with a tax of 20% can be written as:

**80 x 1.2 = $96**

# Positive and Negative Numbers

Whenever you sit down to work out the current state of your finances, you are using positive and negative numbers. Any bills you have to pay are negative; your income is positive. Yet the two may easily be confused. Just as the further a positive number is away from nought, the larger it is, the further a negative number is away from nought, the smaller it is: −1000 is smaller than −10.

If you have two bills to pay, one of $70 and one of $45, you have a total bill of $115. So adding 2 negative numbers together still results in a negative number. Expressed mathematically:

**(−70) + (−45) = −115**  The brackets help to avoid confusion.

But, if you have only one bill of $70, and have been paid $100, you clearly have $30 left over after settling your debts:

**(−70) + 100 = 30**

In this way, you can begin to see that, if the positive value is greater than the negative, you are left with a positive value, and vice versa.

Now, if $30 of the bill for $70 is found to have been a result of overcharging, you must take the $30 away from the $70 to find that you only have $40 to pay:

**(−70) − (−30) = (−70) + 30 = −40**

Now you can also see how 2 minuses make a plus. Perhaps it is simpler than it first appeared after all!

# The Simplest Things in Life

Were you intimidated by the predominantly wordy problems in the self-assessment section? If so, take heart from knowing that a good dose of common sense and logic can be just as helpful as mathematical expertise. Consider the problems below. Would you be able to give an immediate answer?

1. Your boss asks you for a rough evaluation of the results of a survey set up to find out how many teenagers are likely to watch less than 25 hours of television each week. If approximately 30% of those asked were found to spend more than 25 hours a week watching television, and ¾ of a group of 420 teenagers were questioned, what answer would you give your boss?

Don't panic! A rough answer means just that. Try working backward: ¾ of 420 is approximately 300. 30% is roughly ⅓, so about 100 teenagers out of the 300 fall into the more-than-25-hour category. A sensible answer would therefore be:
300 − 100 = 200.

2. You're working to a tight schedule. You've spent just over ⅔ of a 5-day working week on a project, and have got about 15% of it done. You think that the last half, being more complicated, will take double the time. How many weeks do you think it will take to complete the project altogether?

If 15% takes just over ⅔ of a week, then the first 50% equals about 3 lots of this, namely 2 weeks. So the second half takes about 4, and the whole project takes about 6 weeks in total.

# Go It Alone

Now build on the hints in the previous pages to try some problems out for yourself.

1. You inherit a share of the fortune of your uncle's cousin once-removed. Three properties, each valued at $155,000 and 4 cars, each worth about ⅓ of each property, together with shares valued at just under $150,000, form the fortune. If you are entitled to 12%, approximately how much is your inheritance worth?

2. You are trying to ascertain roughly how much cash you will have to live on at the end of the month. You are currently $240 in credit, but have a credit card bill of ⅔ of that to pay at the end of the month, when your salary of $1,250 is paid in. However, you always set 25% of your salary aside to go into your savings account. How much do you reckon on being able to spend?

# Answers

**1.** 27 + (44) = 71 x 3 = (213) − 69 = (144) / (12) = 12 x (7) =   84 − (29) = 55 + (69) = 124.
**2.** $241
**3.** A = 14  B = 9  C = 5

Consider each of the 4 larger triangles in turn; each one is subdivided into 4 smaller ones. Multiply the number at the apex of each large triangle by the number in its base triangle, moving in a clockwise direction. Divide the number you get by the number in the next small base triangle to give the number in the small central triangle.

**4.** C = 5
**5.** 35 seconds

**6.**
**a)** 2.5 (quartered)
**b)** 202 (x3, +1, or +15, +45, +135.)
**c)** 8 (halved, +2, or −32, −16, −8.)
**d)** 95 (−11, −12, −13.)
**e)** 35 (−9, +10, −11, +12.)

**7.** 22.
Cats = 4, mice = 7, dogs = 9

**8.** 297.8 miles

**9.**
**a)** (22 x 2) + 22 = 66
**b)** (44 / 4) + 44 = 55
**c)** (77 + 77) / 7 = 22
**d)** (66 + 6 − 6) / 6 = 11
**e)** (33 x 3) − 33 = 66

**10.** 3
**11.** 324
**12.** One arrow pointing up
**13.** 48
**14.** 323
**15.** 4:30 p.m.

**16.**
**a)** 42 (add 21, working upward on each side)
**b)** 29 (left number + right number = number above left number. Left number + 3 = right number)
**c)** 26 (right number is worth half of the corresponding left number)

**17.** $662
**18.** 7
**19.** 15

**20.** 6 (2 birds per cloud; 3 per sun)

**21.** S = 4, T = 3

**22.** 1 hour 20 minutes (80 minutes)

**Your Score**

0-14 Quite poor – but a little work will soon show a rapid improvement.
15-20 Average. You have made a promising start, so keep going!
21-26 Good. You have obviously found the right approach for dealing with numbers.
27-32 Excellent.

## Go It Alone

**Answers**

**1.** 3 x 150 + 4 x 50 + 150 = 800. Fortune worth about $800,000.
12% = about $\frac{1}{8}$ = about $100,000

**2.** $\frac{2 \times 250}{5}$ = 100. So $150 after credit card. Approximate $1250 to $1200; 75% of which is $900. Left with 900 + 150, about $1050.

# Increase Your Creativity

It's a wonderful moment when a sudden insight flashes into your mind, perhaps solving some troublesome problem or conjuring up an ingenious idea. Creative thinking paves the way for a more exciting, less problematic and often more successful life. See how you fare with the creativity self-assessment tests below. Scoring for all these exercises is on pages 82 and 83.

## Objective Thinking

Consider the list of objects below. Each has its own particular purpose, but your task is to imagine as many other ways as possible that it could be of some use – the more unusual, the better. For example, a submarine would obviously play its part in naval work, but could also serve as a giant incubating chamber for scientific experiments. Dedicate 5 minutes to each object. Feel free to dismantle, rearrange, fill up, transport to an unexpected environment...

1. An empty cassette case.

2. A filing cabinet.

3. Sydney Opera House.

4. A giraffe.

5. A contact lens.

6. A set of scaffolding.

7. A washing-up liquid container.

8. An electric guitar.

9. The Eiffel Tower.

10. The planet Mars.

**ASSESS YOURSELF**

**ASSESS YOURSELF** A

# Playing with Images

The following phrases conjure up a certain kind of visual image. It's up to you to identify up to 3 equivalent phrases that correspond to each image given. You have 3 minutes to find the most apt and original equivalents for each one.

Example

A balloon let loose in the sky.

Could be conceptually synonymous with:

**a.** A twig floating on the ocean.
**b.** A prisoner on being released.
**c.** A painter facing a blank canvas.

Now try these:

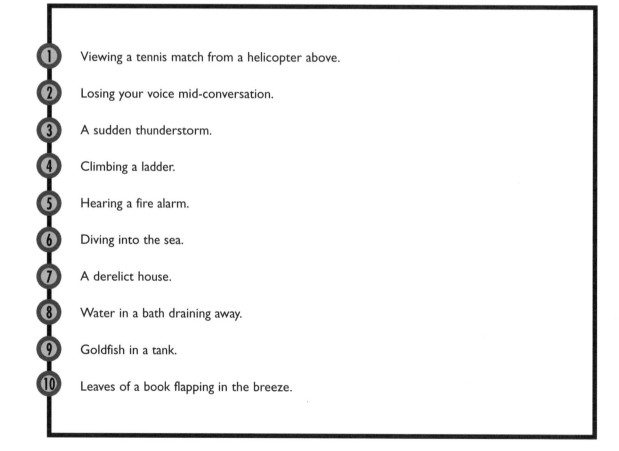

① Viewing a tennis match from a helicopter above.

② Losing your voice mid-conversation.

③ A sudden thunderstorm.

④ Climbing a ladder.

⑤ Hearing a fire alarm.

⑥ Diving into the sea.

⑦ A derelict house.

⑧ Water in a bath draining away.

⑨ Goldfish in a tank.

⑩ Leaves of a book flapping in the breeze.

# Storytime

If you are happier with words than images, you may find that the following task is a better test of your creative spirit. You are allowed up to 300 words to create a smooth, easily understood narrative. It doesn't matter whether it's fact or fiction, just as long as it makes sense! Seems simple? Well, there's one small additional task you have – as many items as possible from the list below must somehow be woven into the thread of your text. The timing is up to you – this is an opportunity for your imagination to roam freely.

Items to include:

1. A toothbrush.
2. A wild animal.
3. A battle – verbal, physical or otherwise.
4. A long journey.
5. A personal catastrophe.
6. Water.
7. A long telephone call.

8. The acquisition of money.
9. Learning a new skill.
10. An art gallery.
11. A tub of cream.
12. A dictionary.
13. The police.
14. A chance encounter.
15. A candle.

# Picture This

Here's another test for the visually creative among you. Study each of the diagrams below for 1 minute, listing as many interpretations as possible of what each one represents.

Whether it is interpreted as producing totally new ideas or combining old ideas in a new way, creativity is something that many of us admire and try to acquire. The exact nature and source of creativity seems to be something of a mystery. Its scientific origin has failed to be precisely determined, and many scientists would say that any definite understanding of exactly what it is will always remain a puzzle.

# What is It?

Some studies suggest that high levels of creativity are related to the way an otherwise typical nervous system functions, rather than to the structure itself. Perhaps it is because of this uncertainty that a diverse display of creativity continues to flourish. If 'rules' about the precise nature of creativity were to be laid down, this might well stifle all kinds of interesting ideas.

There are, however, various factors that we are fairly certain affect creativity. We know that being able to escape preconceptions, conditioning and convention is a key for fresh thought – who said that the average vehicle has to have four wheels? Past experience and knowledge can help us, and often prevents us from making mistakes, but it can also stop us from trying new paths of thought. The very young are generally less inhibited about changing the rules – because they don't yet know what many of them are.

# Early Influences

Childhood plays a vital role in determining our future level of creativity. Everyone is thought to have some creative capacity, so nurturing this skill from an early age can reap huge benefits in later life. The early years can provide a wealth of creative opportunities, and if children are encouraged to explore these actively, rewards are bound to follow later in life. If a parent constantly imposes their view on a child, it will take a very strong-minded child to resist these and forge their own ideas.

Like intelligence, creativity usually lasts into old age – and it may even prolong life. But intelligence is not necessarily related to creativity. Rather than being particularly special, the basic skills that seem to be linked with creativity are actually very ordinary: noticing, recollecting and recognizing. How these are manipulated, however, is where creativity comes in.

# Staying Power

Creative success is predominantly the result of sustained effort and motivation rather than any miraculous power – you cannot become a virtuoso jazz pianist overnight! Technical ability plays no less a part than natural talent and significant displays of creativity are unlikely to appear before a decade of dedicated effort. So, child prodigies do not suddenly acquire their ability from nowhere – they simply started before everybody else! This relentless drive often stems from an endless curiosity, an experimental nature, and an overriding desire to break away from the work of predecessors.

Confidence is a vital factor. It takes courage to break away from convention. As we all know, some of the greatest inventions and ideas of our times were considered insane when they were first put forward.

**PUT IT IN PERSPECTIVE**

PUT IT IN PERSPECTIVE

# Winging It

Improvising solutions to problems that present no obvious explanation is a sure sign of creative thought. However, this obviously requires a great deal of knowledge and experience – pure creativity stems from learning, but is impossible to learn.

Exactly when, where and how a creative idea is born cannot be scientifically predicted. A sudden flash of insight can come into the mind, seemingly from nowhere, although what has probably happened is that the brain has been working away with the idea subconsciously. The creation of an original idea is therefore ongoing. Your initial confrontation with a problem may appear to be unproductive, but this can have the effect of granting your brain unrestricted freedom to play around with it. From this may come that moment of sudden inspiration, culminating in a rational appraisal of the idea. All that remains to be done is to convince others of your genius!

All of this means that no one, regardless of their abilities, can be relied upon to come up with an appropriate idea at exactly the right moment. Nevertheless, a person's overall creativity is still likely to remain relatively consistent.

# Creative Confusion

Creativity can occasionally be confused with ideas that seem original but that actually follow a text-book formula. Editing an existing musical composition, adding bits here and there to make the whole piece appear to be new, is far less creative than composing the piece in the first place. There are countless rules that we all stick to, from how we structure a sentence to how we build a house. Most of us are simply embellishing these when we work, rather than creating the rules themselves.

Whether used to master a particular activity, or merely to cope more efficiently with daily life, an actively creative mind can enhance a range of other mental pursuits. For example, creativity allows much greater abilities of recall. When a topic is approached with an unusual, individual slant, the brain can often access information more quickly. A creative mind is usually a questioning and curious one, in which interest and motivation are kept actively alive and ideas create the desire to discover even more.

# Getting Your Point Across

Creativity is all very well, but unless you can persuade others of your talents, it can easily go unnoticed and unappreciated. People might not have the knowledge necessary to understand your ideas, or may be reluctant to accept new ideas. So, it's often not just a question of being creative, but of being able to communicate concepts to those around you.

# Testing it Out

If allowed room to breathe, creativity is likely to last a lifetime. A conscious effort to maintain your creativity inevitably leads to a life organized in such a way that your creative performance is maximized. If you face each new problem positively, considering how it could be overcome successfully rather than stating that it is simply impossible to solve, creativity will flow much more easily. But patience is essential – creative ideas need time to hatch and grow; they cannot be expected to appear magically whenever you click your fingers!

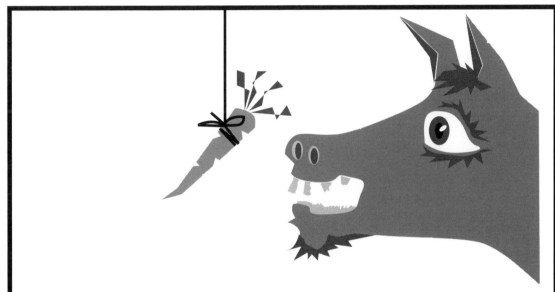

# The Merits of Motivation

Because you need time and the right opportunities to cultivate your creative spirit, no one can be expected to come up with wonderful ideas on a regular basis throughout his or her lifetime. It will always help if you focus your attention on what you enjoy, rather than what you feel you should be attending to. Try to concentrate on a limited area, rather than casually dipping into a medley of subjects. Devotion to a particular area of interest enables the mind to work through ideas that require considerable time and effort to come to fruition.

Motivation is more likely to thrive if the main force of it comes from you, rather than from outside influences. Being genuinely fascinated by something for its own sake, and not simply because of the rewards it can bring, for example, usually brings a greater depth of creativity. Your surroundings, however, do play an important part. Feeling psychologically safe and free to explore can work wonders. Also, while we shouldn't feel too restricted by other people's demands in order to be truly creative, a little support and praise from others can have a dramatic effect.

# The Old and the New

Although you may view creativity as a matter of producing something fresh, give yourself the best possible start by knowing as much as possible about existing ideas before embarking on anything new. A degree of technical knowledge can open your mind up to a wealth of new ideas, sparking off thoughts that may never have occurred to you before. Look at existing information from various perspectives to help you to break away from safe, tried and tested ideas.

Don't let other people's negative reactions automatically interfere with your creative urges. Try to understand and develop your real strengths and talents, and this will give you greater self-confidence. Self-belief and risk-taking form the essence of creative success. Just by looking around you and seeing the range of objects that have originated from someone's creative ingenuity can only serve as an enticement for you to follow suit.

# Breaking Away

Approach each creative challenge on your own terms. Try to break away from existing limitations to develop your own interpretation of each task that you face. Too often people restrict themselves by working within a problem rather than reaching out and beyond it. This is illustrated by the exercise below. You may well be familiar with this puzzle, which asks you to join up all the dots with four straight lines without removing your pen from the paper. The solution is on page 83.

# Brainstorming

Brainstorming serves as a tremendous aid in improving creativity; decide whether you prefer to do it on your own or with other people. Try simply noting down any thought and association that comes to mind when you focus on a specific task – no matter how bizarre it might seem. You may find that the mere act of writing down the relevant issue in the middle of a blank piece of paper, and creating a web of related ideas branching out from this produces more than enough ideas ready to pursue. Or, if you are working with others, you might simply throw ideas around out loud – perhaps playing word association games and so on. Brainstorming itself needn't be a lengthy process – it is the development of each thought that may take some time.

Whether you are alone or generating ideas with others, relax and let your ideas flow. Speaking continuously, simply saying whatever springs to mind, activates the brain encouraging ideas. Whether your words contain the beginnings of a promising idea, or merely show that no ideas are forthcoming, is irrelevant – take heart from knowing that even the most creative mind lapses every now and again!

# In brainstorming sessions, don't:

- **stop to worry whether what you are saying is grammatical or beautifully expressed**

- **feel that you have to justify every thought – in the early stages, simply the fact that you have come up with it yourself makes an idea justifiable; it is only later, after further deliberation, than you need to defend it against possible opposition.**

Develop your thoughts as you experience them, as opposed to relating them or writing them down later. Thinking and speaking simultaneously can enable a chain of thoughts to unwind and gradually move toward its full potential. Regardless of whether your chosen instrument is a pen or a paintbrush, music or science, a positive approach and determination help to maximize success. Leave it to others to set the limits and restrictions – telling yourself you can't do it only adds to your obstacles. Don't be your own worst enemy!

# S SOLUTIONS

## Objective Thinking

**Your Score**

Only you, or preferably an unbiased volunteer, can judge the quality of your responses. However, as a general guide:

0-4 uses for each object: Poor. You probably just need to relax more and your creative ideas will flow more readily.
5-8: Good. You are obviously used to looking at things from all kinds of angles.
Above 8: Excellent.

## Playing with Images

**Scoring**

Award yourself points as follows (or get an obliging friend to help):

0 for failing to respond, or producing an inappropriate, unrelated response.
1 for an appropriate but unoriginal answer (example response: a)
2 points for an appropriate and more original answer (example response: b)
3 points for an appropriate and highly original, imaginative answer (example response: c)

0-40: Poor. Again, you'll find this much easier if you relax and stop looking for the 'right' answer.
41-65: Good. You've got good creative potential but you tend to hold back. Dare to be more adventurous with your ideas!
66-90: Excellent.

# Storytime

### Scoring
That helpful friend will come in handy again! Starting with a score of 15, deduct one point for the omission of each item. Now award a score out of 5 (5 being the best) for:

a. How well the text flows and general clarity.
b. Degree of interest/amusement/enjoyment derived from your story.
c. Level of original and imaginative thought.

### Your Score
0-16: Poor. Your creative muscles just need a bit of exercise.
17-23: Good. Now see how much further you can take your creative ideas.
24-30: Excellent.

# Picture This

### Your Score.
For each diagram:
0-3 interpretations: Poor.
4-6: Good.
7 or over: Excellent.

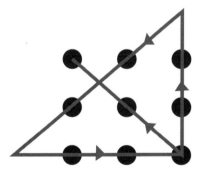

# Breaking Away
Most people approach this first by restricting the lines to the square itself; the solution demands that the pen breaks away from the confines of the square. Make sure that, whenever you face a new challenge, you don't always trap yourself within a limiting square.

# Making Better Decisions

To be or not to be? To do or not to do? To go or not to go? Every day, a multitude of decisions need to be taken, ranging from which side of the bed to get out of (easier if your bed lies next to the wall!) to deciding to buy a house. Use this self-assessment section to discover which kind of decision-maker you are. Only, however, if you decide that you want to.

## Well, I'm Not Too Sure...

Imagine yourself in each of the following situations. Your task is to note which of the reactions you consider yourself most likely to follow. Be honest – you are the only judge.

**1**

You drop in to say hello to the person who lives next door. When asked if you would like a drink, do you say:

a. Only if you're making one.
b. I'd love a coffee.
c. Yes, please.

Your roommate says that he feels like cooking a special supper, and asks you what you would like. Do you:

**a.** Ask what's in the fridge.
**b.** Say it's up to him.
**c.** Present him with a specific recipe.

You're planning to go abroad with a group of friends for a couple of weeks. When someone asks you where you'd like to go, do you:

**a.** Say you have no ideas, or just name the first country that comes into your head.
**b.** Suggest a place visited by a friend or work colleague last year, which they said was very pleasant.
**c.** Hunt around and look in various brochures before making your suggestions.

You and some friends are trying to decide where to go one Saturday evening. Do you decide to:

**a.** Organize the party, and start ringing venues up to get details about what's on offer.
**b.** Go along with whatever the others decide.
**c.** Make a few half-hearted suggestions.

After a shopping trip, you discover that the shirt you bought has a hole under the collar. Do you:

**a.** Take it straight back.
**b.** Make a mental note to do something about it sometime.
**c.** Put it down to bad luck and leave it to rot in your wardrobe.

**ASSESS YOURSELF**

**ASSESS YOURSELF**

You're uncomfortable in your current long-standing relationship and are wondering how to resolve things. Do you:

**a.** Wait and see what happens.
**b.** Sit down with your partner to have a serious talk and get things sorted out.
**c.** Pack your bags and move out.

During one evening at home, the noise made by the family next door is driving you crazy. Do you:

**a.** Spend so long wondering about whether to go round and complain that the noise eventually stops without any interference.
**b.** Agree with your housemate that it would be a good idea for someone, namely her, to go and complain.
**c.** Decide to give it another 20 minutes, and if it's still unbearable, go round yourself.

A business acquaintance offers you a – more challenging – job out of the blue. Do you:

**a.** Immediately try to find out more about it.
**b.** Refuse at once, sticking with your current job for fear of change.
**c.** Put off making a choice, asking for more time to think it over.

Once again, you find yourself struggling with an awkward lock on the front door. Do you:

**a.** Remind yourself to get a locksmith round next week.
**b.** Grumble slightly, then forget about it until you next find yourself trying to get into the house.
**c.** Declare that you can't stand this any more, and get it sorted out immediately.

The telephone rings when you're sitting down with your family at home. Do you:

**a.** Get up and answer it straight away.
**b.** Ask if you should answer it or is someone else going to?
**c.** Wait to be asked to answer it.

You open the front door and are greeted by a salesman, who immediately tries to sell you goods you're really not interested in. Do you:

**a.** Tell him you're not interested and shut the door.
**b.** Say half-heartedly that you're not really sure.
**c.** End up being persuaded to buy a multitude of things you will never use.

You are asked to do something about a problem that has cropped up at work which requires considerable investigation. Do you:

**a.** Hope that it will improve without undue interference.
**b.** Start a detailed survey to pinpoint the cause and take the appropriate action.
**c.** Tackle some of the superficial symptoms ineffectually rather than addressing the root cause.

You suspect that the house next door is being broken into after hearing a series of mysterious noises. Do you:

**a.** Ring for the police straight away.
**b.** Panic, which is of little help to anyone.
**c.** Go and tell someone else of your suspicions, leaving it up to them to take any action.

**ASSESS YOURSELF**

**ASSESS YOURSELF**

**14**

You've saved up for a long time to buy a car. The day has finally arrived, but you find yourself torn between two models. Do you:

**a.** Ask the salesman for his opinion.
**b.** Toss a coin to decide.
**c.** Eventually pick one of the models yourself.

**15**

You're shopping for a pair of shoes to wear to your sister's wedding, and end up finding two pairs that you're really keen on. Do you:

**a.** Buy both, and decide which pair to wear on the big day.
**b.** Come home empty-handed, unable to choose which pair to buy.
**c.** Rationally choose the pair you think you'll get most use out of.

**16**

Your generous aunt asks you what you would like for your birthday. Do you:

**a.** Say it's up to her – you can't think of any particular thing.
**b.** Finally come up with something you know you'll really appreciate.
**c.** Give her a choice of items off the top of your head.

**17**

The day of your hairdresser's appointment arrives, and you turn up in the mood for a change of style. In the end, do you:

**a.** Leave it all up to your hairdresser.
**b.** Just ask for a trim – again.
**c.** Describe the different style you want in precise detail.

**18**

You're not too sure what to do on your longed-for day off. Do you:

**a.** Set about drawing up a plan of action, and stick to it.
**b.** Have a marathon couch-potato session.
**c.** Pass the day without knowing what you've done.

An important decision concerning the siting of a new factory is under discussion at work. When asked for your professional opinion, do you:

**a.** Pick a particular location because it seems a popular choice with everyone else.
**b.** Compile a list detailing the merits of each site, and make your decision based on this.
**c.** Select the location closest to your home.

During a hectic weekend of apartment-hunting, you've narrowed the options down to three. Do you choose:

**a.** The place with the nicest view.
**b.** The apartment without any structural problems.
**c.** The apartment that comes complete with fitted carpets.

You're feeling rather tired and are looking forward to an early night when a friend calls, asking you to go to a party with her. Do you:

**a.** Explain politely that you've decided to stay in.
**b.** Ask your friend to call back half an hour later, when you will have made up your mind.
**c.** Let yourself be persuaded, against your better judgement.

You've been invited out on a picnic, but when the day arrives, your fears that the people who are going will not get on well together come to the fore, and you feel reluctant to go. Do you:

**a.** Go along anyway, attempting to dismiss your fears.
**b.** Ring up and cancel.
**c.** Turn up, armed with some games that you could play if the conversation gets really hard-going.

**ASSESS YOURSELF**

**ASSESS YOURSELF**

**ASSESS YOURSELF**

**23**

A major corporate decision is left to you. You have access to detailed statistical data and surveys of public opinion. Do you make your decision on the basis of:

**a.** What you can deduce from the available data, despite feeling that your understanding of the statistics is somewhat cloudy.
**b.** The advice of others, as you don't want to be unpopular.
**c.** Your own judgement, having sought explanations for anything that you found unclear.

**24**

A friend telephones you in a state of panic after discovering that her kitchen is flooded. Do you:

**a.** Try to stop yourself from panicking and rush round at once, forgetting in the rush to take your buckets along.
**b.** Ask if she's rung for a plumber, offering calming advice before dashing over to give constructive help.
**c.** Say, 'So what do you think I can do about it?'

**25**

When completing questionnaires, do you often:

**a.** Tick the don't know/can't be sure boxes.
**b.** Respond with a definite yes or no.
**c.** Ask others nearby what they think.

**26**

You're going to an auction that promises to offer an intriguing selection of curiosities. Do you:

**a.** Set yourself a spending limit and stick to it.
**b.** End up buying a variety of junk despite your good intentions.
**c.** Return empty-handed – you always seemed to miss your chance.

You notice a mysterious clunking noise coming from the engine of your car when you are speeding along the open road on a long journey. Do you:

**a.** Carry on as before until you reach your destination, hoping it will go away.
**b.** Slow down a little, listening carefully for a while before turning off somewhere to seek assistance.
**c.** Nearly cause an accident in your panic to get off the road.

You're considering taking an evening class. After browsing through a list of what is on offer, do you:

**a.** Finally decide on a course that really appeals to you, weighing up the possible future benefits.
**b.** Feel so overwhelmed by the choice that you put the list aside, but when you do choose you discover it's too late to enrol.
**c.** Agree to enrol on a course that your friend has urged you to do with him.

At work, each member of your department has been asked to compile a report on a different aspect of the company. A list of the various aspects is circulated, from which you are to choose the one that appeals to you. Do you:

**a.** Claim first pick, having rushed to choose before anyone else has made up their mind.
**b.** Wait until last, when all except one has been selected.
**c.** While most options are still up for grabs, consider which topic you know most about.

You suddenly realize that you've lost a valuable watch of great sentimental value. Do you:

**a.** Panic, getting very upset and proceeding to accuse anyone near you of moving/stealing it.
**b.** Make yourself relax before conducting a meticulous search.
**c.** Hope that it will turn up later.

**ASSESS YOURSELF**

**ASSESS YOURSELF**

Research has so far failed to provide conclusive evidence about the precise areas of the brain responsible for judgement and decision-making – especially intuitive, gut-reaction decision-making. In some 'decisions', the brain is not even consciously involved. For instance, removing a finger that is being burned from a scalding surface happens instantaneously, and is known as a reflex reaction. As well as taking vital unconscious 'decisions' such as this in order for survival, the same sensory pathways in the nervous system are claimed to have some influence over our emotions. Here, the way that we behave is largely dictated by a constant stream of decisions that demand more conscious consideration. These types of decision vary greatly – from what to have for lunch to whether or not to make hundreds of people redundant. The amount of attention that you give to each should obviously be very different.

# Taking Responsibility

The making of a decision arises only when the need to do so is recognized in the first place. So, the greater your responsibilities, whether at home or at work, the more dilemmas you will need to resolve. A good decision often requires clarification of a specific objective – deciding to build a new supermarket on a particularly cheap plot of land is futile if public access is limited.

A decision is very rarely thought to be ideal by all the parties involved – what's better for one party may well be detrimental to another. Wise decisions try to ensure that the overall benefits outweigh the costs and come to some sort of thoughtful compromise.

# Deciding What to Decide On

How a problem is to be addressed can determine the direction a decision takes. Action can be immediate or delayed, taken either to prevent a certain situation from occurring, or correcting the results later. Acting with an astute mind, anticipating what may happen before it actually does, can relieve much of the pressure of what may otherwise require a far more difficult decision. The best decisions are geared not so much to the perfect outcome as to the best use of the available resources. However well judged the decision, it doesn't mean that a miracle will follow.

# Deciding Factors

Obviously, your personality strongly affects your style of decision-making. If you enjoy risk-taking, your decisions will differ dramatically from those made by someone who can never bear to leave anything to chance. So too will your success rate – a determination to be a high-achiever frequently dictates the gambles you decide to take. The same goes for self-confidence. Trusting your instincts and convictions and accepting personal responsibility enables decisions to be taken much faster. Self-doubt is disastrous, as is obstinately sticking to your view without listening to any advice.

You must decide what type of approach is best for the issue in question. The decision-maker who always grabs too quickly at an answer and then spends all their time justifying it might have directed their energies more constructively into reviewing different options in the first place. The logical approach commonly adopted by children can prove highly fruitful: if I did this, then that would happen, which would mean that such-and-such would occur. Unfortunately, such a rational chain of thought is too often considered inferior to more instantaneous decision-making, where the pressures of time render such deliberation unfeasible.

Having said this, intuition certainly has a vital role to play in all kinds of day-to-day decisions. The absence of conscious thought often makes it very difficult to explain exactly what has prompted a particular decision. But just because you cannot fully justify a certain decision does not necessarily mean that it should be dismissed. Technological and scientific advances place more and more emphasis on knowing exactly why you did something, but on an everyday basis, intuitive decisions are invaluable – and have an uncanny tendency to prove themselves right.

# Natural Talents

Your natural creativity will strongly influence your approach. If your views are rather narrow and blinkered, you are less likely to make effective decisions. An original, refreshing outlook often produces greater understanding of a problem, allowing the most appropriate decision to be made – if you don't understand all the options available, how can you hope to select the right one?

Another powerful influence is stress, which can have a disastrous effect on the most accomplished decision-maker. The pressures of time, the irritability stemming from fatigue, the draining effects of illness – all can produce poor judgements. The negative feelings that stress produces can also make a bad decision worse by clouding your thinking, making you incapable of taking the right action to try to make things better.

**PUT IT IN PERSPECTIVE**

# Top Decision-making Tips

The need to make a decision often stems from a specific problem. Establishing the root cause of the problem, and that it really does exist, improves your understanding of the situation, enabling the most appropriate action to be taken.

**2**

Ascertain the importance of your dilemma in order to make a decision of an appropriate scale. Under or over-reacting can have disastrous or simply timewasting consequences.

**3**

Good decisions usually spring from being fully armed with all the facts. Be suspicious of potentially misleading statistics or biased 'experts'.

**4**

Although statistical data may be misleading, don't automatically be afraid to use it because of this, or because of a fear of numbers. It can provide valuable insights into a situation, so if you lack the confidence to deal with it, don't be afraid to seek advice from someone who doesn't.

Establish exactly what you hope to achieve from each decision you make before making it. Identifying a precise objective helps you to consider appropriate options and seek the best outcome.

Avoid being rushed into making a choice whenever possible, especially if you feel that this is impairing your judgement. It can be more beneficial to respond by saying 'can I get back to you?' or 'this isn't a good time' rather than making a hasty decision simply to please someone. Of course, you need to decide whether you are delaying the decision from a conscientious need to consider it further, or just because you are indecisive.

If you really are undecided, try jotting down the pros and cons. You may even discover that the grounds for deciding to take action are weak, and that no decision needs to be taken after all!

Have the confidence to make bold decisions – don't follow conventional patterns just for the sake of it. When you have to face the consequences of any decision you make, it may as will be one you truly believe in.

A fear of questioning other people's decisions can restrict your own decision-making abilities. A creative and original approach to a problem encourages a fresh outlook, providing the means to make wiser, more informed decisions.

**TEST IT OUT**

**TEST IT OUT** T

It is important to stress the potential rewards of being open-minded, willing to examine the grounds for, and effects of, a decision from all viewpoints. Concentrate on seeking the most acceptable solution for everybody, not simply opting for the easiest choice now, which might prove disastrous in the long-run.

In a business environment, attempting to thrash out every conceivable problem yourself is not advisable. Deciding which decisions to delegate, and to whom, can produce far better results. This makes best use of different people's areas of expertise and means that you can focus your attentions fully on particular decisions, rather than tackling all of them in a rush.

Don't be afraid to listen to the opinions of others, but avoid total subordination. People are all too willing to give their advice, but remember that, if it's your decision, you will ultimately have to take the responsibility for it.

If you cannot think what options are open to you, let alone pick one, brainstorming may enable you to reach an acceptable solution. This helps avoid unprofitable bouts of panic: 'Help! What am I going to do?'

**14**

Respect and listen to your intuition.

# Do Good Decisions Always Take Time?

Not necessarily. Shrewd, quick-witted thinking can be more effective than hours spent laboriously considering all the options. Only you know what suits you. If you are a spur-of-the-moment, decisive thinker, you are unlikely to gain much benefit from carefully dissecting every option open to you – chances are, you are aware of them already. However, if you feel that your decision-making process is more a matter of continually changing your mind over and over again because of sheer indecision, it's up to you to put a stop to it. Be firm, make that decision, and then stick with it.

# The Good and the Bad

A good decision leaves the situation better than it was before – it's as simple as that. The process you went through may well have been:

- Identifying the problem, and its cause

- Generating various possible options and appraising the relative virtues of each one

- Choosing an option and putting it into practice

- Monitoring the results.

**TEST IT OUT**

**TEST IT OUT** **T**

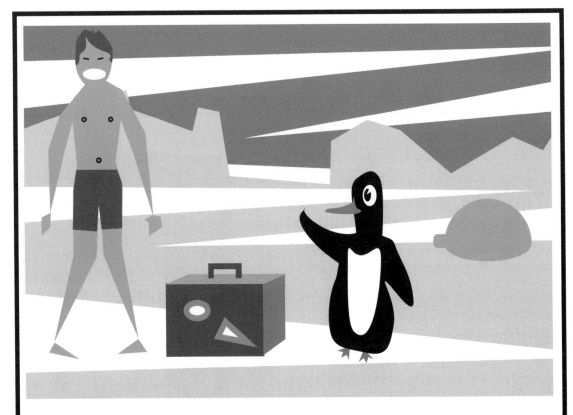

# Making the Most of a Bad Decision

So, when you come to monitor the results, what can you do if your decision has gone horribly wrong? Don't deny further responsibility or allow it to dent your self-confidence – this could be a potentially enriching opportunity to learn something. It is too easy to view a bad outcome as a lost investment – the investment being time, difficult soul-searching and even a financial loss. Try, if you can, to salvage something from the situation, but if it is a total disaster, don't be afraid to admit that it is, and start again from scratch. Do not stick with something just because you expended a lot of energy on it in the first place; that way, things will go from bad to worse. Take responsibility and do what you can to get things back on the right path.

# Self-assessment quiz

## Scoring

| | a. | b. | c. | | a. | b. | c. |
|---|---|---|---|---|---|---|---|
| 1. | 0 | 2 | 1 | 16. | 0 | 2 | 1 |
| 2. | 1 | 0 | 2 | 17. | 0 | 1 | 2 |
| 3. | 0 | 1 | 2 | 18. | 2 | 1 | 0 |
| 4. | 2 | 0 | 1 | 19. | 1 | 2 | 0 |
| 5. | 2 | 1 | 0 | 20. | 0 | 2 | 1 |
| 6. | 0 | 2 | 1 | 21. | 2 | 1 | 0 |
| 7. | 0 | 1 | 2 | 22. | 0 | 1 | 2 |
| 8. | 2 | 1 | 0 | 23. | 1 | 0 | 2 |
| 9. | 1 | 0 | 2 | 24. | 1 | 2 | 0 |
| 10. | 2 | 1 | 0 | 25. | 1 | 2 | 0 |
| 11. | 2 | 1 | 0 | 26. | 2 | 1 | 0 |
| 12. | 0 | 2 | 1 | 27. | 0 | 2 | 1 |
| 13. | 2 | 0 | 1 | 28. | 2 | 0 | 1 |
| 14. | 0 | 1 | 2 | 29. | 1 | 0 | 2 |
| 15. | 1 | 0 | 2 | 30. | 0 | 2 | 1 |

## Your Score

0-20 You appear reluctant to take decisions, and rely heavily on the judgement of others. Learn to have faith in yourself for once. Be careful not to rush into making a decision just to please someone else; a little more thought now will have much better results later. You could be taking consideration for others too far – sometimes you need to think harder about what you would like.

21-40 You seem to have achieved a good balance between deciding what's best for you and what's best for others. A fear of being wrong may be preventing you from trusting your own instincts more, often preferring to take the safe option rather than going it alone on a matter of some controversy. Take care not to feel pressured – your basic decision-making skills are sound, but may be greatly improved by more thorough exploration of the options open to you. Don't be afraid to ask for advice if you need it.

41-60 You certainly know what you want in life! The assertive confidence you have in yourself helps you to make decisions regardless of what others are pushing you to do. Although you may gain respect for this, watch out for being too self-opinionated, and unwilling to take notice of other people's advice. You are generally able to make a reasoned judgement of a situation, without feeling the need to rush into an inaccurate but prompt decision.

**ASSESS YOURSELF**

# The Art of Communication

## Self-assessment

It's impossible to survive without communicating with those around you, whether you're ordering a takeaway or negotiating a crucial business deal. Assess your communication skills by considering the points raised below. Circle the number which you consider to be most appropriate, with 1 representing agreement, 2 sometimes/can't be sure and 3 disagreement.

---

1. I often find myself unable to think of something to say to someone.
           1    2    3

2. When I disagree with someone, the conversation normally ends in an argument.
           1    2    3

3. I don't find it very easy to approach a stranger and start a conversation.
           1    2    3

4. Before now, I have felt that people are prejudiced against me because of the image I project.
           1    2    3

5. I tend to avoid making eye contact, particularly when addressing those in a superior position.
           1    2    3

6. I have been known to raise my voice and speak slower when trying to make myself understood to people who don't speak my language.
           1    2    3

7. I am reluctant to go to parties where I don't know many of the guests as I usually end up standing on my own.
           1    2    3

8. I find it difficult to persuade others to agree with my way of thinking.
           1    2    3

9. Sometimes, I suspect that whoever I'm talking to is paying little attention to what I'm saying.
           1    2    3

10. I tend to cross my legs and fold my arms when sitting down.
           1    2    3

11. I'm known more as a talker than a listener.
           1    2    3

**12.** I prefer talking about myself than finding out about other people.

        1    2    3

**13.** If I pass someone I know vaguely in the street, I usually wait for them to say hello.

        1    2    3

**14.** People can take me or leave me – I'm not prepared to change myself for anyone.

        1    2    3

**15.** I'm really quite shy, although strangers tend to mistake this for sullenness.

        1    2    3

**16.** I have an unfortunate tendency to say the wrong thing at the wrong time.

        1    2    3

**17.** I prefer to launch straight into a debate, rather than planning what I want to say first.

        1    2    3

**18.** I have come unstuck in job interviews before now, rambling on and on, not knowing what I am saying or when to stop.

        1    2    3

**19.** I feel uneasy in unfamiliar social situations, and have no idea what to say.

        1    2    3

**20.** I have been known to upset people unintentionally when what I say doesn't come out quite as I meant it to.

        1    2    3

**21.** I don't like using the telephone as I feel pressured into talking, often unable to get my point across properly.

        1    2    3

**22.** I'm not normally the one who is nominated to be spokesperson when something important needs to be said.

        1    2    3

**23.** If I've delegated a task to someone else, it tends not to be carried out exactly as I would like, because my instructions aren't very clear.

        1    2    3

**24.** I usually grab whatever clothes are at hand, rather than carefully considering what would be most appropriate.

        1    2    3

**25.** I have quite a small, select circle of friends, as people don't approach me very often.

        1    2    3

**26.** I can become so involved in talking about myself that I forget that anyone else is there.

        1   2 3

**27.** I always say precisely what I think, regardless of who I'm talking to.

        1    2    3

**28.** I can talk to someone for hours, then come away without knowing anything about them.

        1    2    3

**29.** I much prefer to let other people do the talking.

        1    2    3

**30.** Sometimes I upset people, not quite realizing how or why.

        1    2    3

**ASSESS YOURSELF**

**ASSESS YOURSELF**

**ASSESS YOURSELF**

# Would You... or Wouldn't You?

Now consider each of the situations described below, selecting the action you (honestly!) consider yourself most likely to take.

**1**

You've been working on a somewhat controversial idea which you hope will earn you a pay rise as it's aimed at increasing your company's turnover. When you next speak to your boss, do you:

**a.** Launch into explaining your idea confidently, saying how inefficient you think the company is at present.
**b.** Request a convenient time to propose your idea, outlining its possible future benefits.
**c.** Fail to mention it at all, as you doubt that the boss will listen to you anyway.

**2**

You suddenly find that you are the only one talking in a room full of people. Is this most likely to be because:

**a.** Your words and generally appealing manner have captured everybody's attention.
**b.** You are so absorbed by what you are saying that you have failed to notice the call for silence.
**c.** Everyone else has fallen asleep.

**3**

At a party, you notice a stranger who you would like to start talking to. To attract his or her attention, do you:

**a.** Ask the host to introduce you, feeling too shy to wander over yourself.
**b.** Walk over confidently and start elaborating on your life history.
**c.** Carefully make eye contact, waiting for a positive response before initiating a conversation.

**4**

The day of an important business interview arrives. When you get ready, do you:

**a.** Put on the clothes you selected last night, neatly pressed and hung up, ready for action.
**b.** Reach for the suit you find buried in the back of your wardrobe, only to discover you have no time left to replace the missing button.
**c.** Throw anything on, as long as it's clean.

**5**

You discover that the television you have just purchased is faulty. Do you:

**a.** Take it back to the retailer, or phone them, explaining your problem and politely request a prompt repair or exchange.
**b.** Ask a friend if they will approach the retailer as you don't get very far when complaining.
**c.** End up being fobbed off by the retailer and putting up with the faulty TV.

**6**

You are trying to convert an acquaintance to your way of thinking during a heated debate. When you reach the end of the discussion, is it most likely that:

**a.** Your acquaintance has stormed off in a huff, after you insulted her for her beliefs.
**b.** You both recognize that the other has a valid point, but agree to differ.
**c.** Your acquaintance has relinquished her argument, finally agreeing with yours.

**7**

A mock trial during a business training weekend requires you to defend the accused despite your underlying conviction of his guilt. Do you:

**a.** Present a weak case, convincing the jury more of your incompetence than the innocence of the accused.
**b.** Argue the case with courage and conviction, seizing solely on the evidence that backs up your position.
**c.** Have a good stab at it, but end up presenting a confused and unduly complicated argument.

**ASSESS YOURSELF**

**ASSESS YOURSELF** Ⓐ

**ASSESS YOURSELF**

**8**

Which do you consider to be of most importance when first attempting to impress a potential employer?

**a.** Being well read.
**b.** An appropriately smart appearance.
**c.** How many impressive people you know.

**9**

You're trying to convince an audience of the validity of your argument during a public speech. To help achieve your aim, do you end up:

**a.** Following a rational line of thought, gradually building up the evidence for your point of view in order to minimize any disagreements.
**b.** Delivering a carefully rehearsed speech, but coming unstuck and confused when questioned.
**c.** Speaking louder and louder, in the hope that your confidence and sheer volume will disguise the weaknesses of your argument.

**10**

You wish to approach your rather daunting boss to ask for a well-deserved raise. Do you:

**a.** Chatter on about why you should get a raise without letting your boss get a word in.
**b.** Bluntly deliver your request, presenting an ultimatum that backfires against you.
**c.** Politely reason with your boss, explaining your justification to your advantage.

**11**

You're trying to negotiate the price and conditions for which a reputable electrician will rewire your house. Do you:

**a.** Flatly declare that you consider the estimate to be unreasonable, informing the electrician that she can take it or leave it – she leaves it.
**b.** Reach a compromise whereby both you and the electrician come to an amicable agreement.
**c.** Allow yourself to be manipulated by the electrician, agreeing without too much resistance to pay a higher price than you would like to.

Plans to build a huge supermarket that would severely disrupt life near your home are put forward. You greet them with strong opposition. Do you voice your concerns by:

**a.** Writing a persuasive letter to a local political figure, attached to a weighty petition that you have organized.
**b.** Ruthlessly hunt down the proposers of the plan, hysterically threatening them with the future action you are prepared to take.
**c.** Sell up before the construction team starts to arrive.

During the course of your professional duties, you find yourself having to make several employees redundant. Do you:

**a.** Shirk responsibility, attempting to nominate someone else to tell them – you'll only say it all wrong.
**b.** Flatly inform the workers of their misfortune, preferring to stick to the facts to avoid getting too personally involved.
**c.** Deliver the news as kindly as possible, offering what few words of comfort you can.

One of your housemates has an annoying but unnecessary habit that is seriously frustrating you. Do you:

**a.** Drop unsubtle hints until your grievance has been noted.
**b.** Explain directly to your housemate that you don't want to start an argument, but...
**c.** Start plaguing your housemate with an equally annoying habit of your own.

You've felt yourself drifting away from your partner for some time, but have been reluctant to admit it. When your partner broaches the subject and asks exactly what's wrong, do you:

**a.** Say nothing's wrong – you've just been feeling a bit down lately.
**b.** Vent your frustration, so you end up having a massive row that achieves nothing.
**c.** Awkwardly explain that you think you need to talk, trying to couch your feelings in the clearest, kindest manner.

**ASSESS YOURSELF**

This is the age of advanced technological communication, but what about relating to people on a personal level? It seems that we all have some way to go where this skill is concerned. Whether causing major corporate problems, or needlessly provoking a petty argument, communication problems are all around us. The difficulties are intensified when cultural and social differences come to the fore.

The complexity inherent in even the most basic conversation – where a grammatically clear and logical word sequence must be formed, delivered, understood and appropriately responded to within a pretty brief timespan – is rarely considered. And it is not just words that must be taken into account. Gestures, facial expression, body language, tone of voice – and even clothes and hairstyle – are all-important, and when they contradict whatever is being said this can cause enormous confusion. We all know that stressing one word rather than another can alter the message we are putting across.

# Tools of the Trade

The fact that there are so many tools at your disposal when you are relating to others makes communication an exciting, varied experience. The vocal chords and mouth can produce a huge range of sounds, complemented by all kinds of facial movements and expressions: dilation of the pupils, blushing, smiling, crying...

Your eyes say a great deal about you, from silently expressing a welcome to revealing a guilty secret. Conversation benefits greatly from frequent eye contact, whether demonstrating interest, enforcing opinions, or indicating the need for a response. But a careful balance is vital to ensure the comfort of all parties. When eye contact is non-existent, people may think that you really find inspecting your fingernails much more interesting than talking to them. But people will recoil with discomfort if you fix them eyeball to eyeball throughout an entire conversation.

The messages your clothes send out are easier to control, which is fortunate because they can have a very powerful impact, revealing all kinds of things about your attitudes and lifestyle. Your clothes and self-presentation can also reveal a great deal about your creative side, long before you've had a chance to say anything about your ideas. Success in life frequently stems from an ability to tailor this stream of verbal and non-verbal messages to a particular environment.

# A Key to Success

Considering how easily an ordinary conversation between two people can falter, when this is magnified, for example, within a large company, the results can be disastrous. Failure to inform certain departments in a company of whatever is going on could prevent adequate general discussion of a business' problems, so a single communication problem can gather a catastrophic momentum. Used positively, to build bridges toward others, the rewards of effective communication will be great and it can certainly be a key to business success. Consider the amount of job specifications asking for a 'good telephone manner' or 'excellent interpersonal skills.'

# Assert Yourself

All of us would benefit from communicating more assertively – stating what we want clearly and listening carefully to what others want. Assertive does not mean domineering. It is merely a way of letting people know where they stand and allowing everyone to get what they want from a situation – in other words, good communication.

# T TEST IT OUT

Establishing an initial rapport with people is vital for easy, enjoyable conversation. Judge your greeting carefully. Although some countries are renowned for their very physical greetings, embracing a stranger in the middle of the street is unlikely to communicate a good impression anywhere in the world.

# At Ease!

Early signs of warmth and friendliness encourage all parties to feel instantly at ease. This emotional comfort fosters trust, which in turn brings much smoother discourse. Minimizing disruptions gives each speaker more of a chance – don't keep asking someone if they want more coffee when they are in mid-sentence! Introducing an amusing note is always a good way to dissolve tensions, but be careful to strike the right tone – the amusing tales you tell your closest friends may not be appreciated by your bank manager. Conversely, try to avoid being so quiet that you are thought to be hostile or aloof. Remember, even if you can't think of anything to say, smiling and making encouraging noises always helps, and you may find that this helps your shyness to ebb away naturally as you ease yourself gently into the conversation.

# What Now?

As the conversation progresses, take into account the following points:

Be aware of how you are judging people – and how they are judging you. Signals of disapproval that you may send out unconsciously may instigate a ro w. Dressing to suit the situation may also bring rewa rds.

**2**

Adapting your language and manner, as well as your clothes, to the person you are dealing with is considerate and establishes a good understanding between you. If you get it wrong, you can build an immediate barrier that is very difficult to break down. This isn't to say that your conduct should constantly mirror that of others around you - just be aware of how you can get along with others more sensitively.

**3**

What you don't say can be as important as what you do. Attentive listening, questioning others rather than talking continually about yourself, is always appreciated. By concentrating closely on what is being said to you, you can find yourself in a better position to respond in the most effective manner. Remember that people naturally enjoy talking about themselves – a willingness to listen will win you many friends.

**4**

Consider other people's reactions to you in order to assess how well you are communicating. If all you are met with is a yawn (or even a snore!), the chances are your words are not exciting much interest. But don't just notice it and feel discouraged or angry – act on the feedback you receive.

**TEST IT OUT**

**TEST IT OUT** **T**

**5**

As to the feedback you give out, use it to your advantage. Communicate your interest by smiling, nodding, making eye contact and using positive words of encouragement. Crossing your arms and legs creates a body-language barrier; it is a defensive position indicative of unease and a reluctance to listen. Open yourself up to others and they will respond in kind.

**6**

To help gain and sustain people's attention, vary the pitch and tone of your voice. A dull and monotonous monologue, lacking any variety of expression, does little to win people over. Also, don't bombard people with an endless stream of words. Momentary pauses, attending to minor interruptions from others, and supporting your argument with gestures, are all-important when striving to become a successful communicator.

**7**

If arguing a particular point, little is gained by adapting a louder, more aggressive voice. This often simply alienates you from others. A raised voice indicates anger and a desire to dominate, inevitably leading to anger on the other side too. A gently persuasive, coherent argument is more likely to produce the result you desire.

**8**

Maintaining clarity is essential for communicative success. Think clearly before speaking so that you are easily understood. A succinct argument can be more powerful than a rambling, illogical lecture. Good articulation and an air of certainty are greatly beneficial. If you don't know what you mean, how can you expect anyone else to? Devising a plan outlining what you want to communicate to someone during an important conversation could be useful, while simultaneously boosting your confidence.

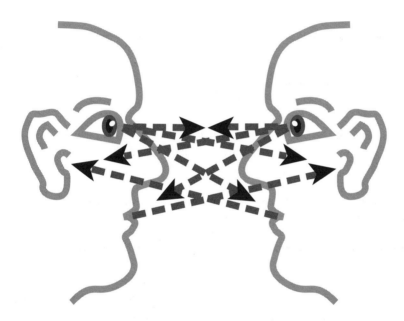

# Negotiating Skills

Successful negotiation involves establishing a degree of persuasive, not overbearing, influence. A good rapport provides a better foundation on which to construct a framework for negotiation. During the discussion, act assertively but avoid aggression. Restrain any desire to score points by shouting, making unpleasant or sarcastic remarks or trying to appear superior. Attempts to appease and reason with your listener will nearly always be more productive. Your confident manner can be enhanced by friendly gestures. This attracts more respect and co-operation than a fiercely dominant approach. As always, regular eye contact enforces your viewpoint and expresses your confidence and determination. It is important to physically demonstrate your interest and assertion, while taking care not to emit an overwhelming stubborness.

**TEST IT OUT**

**TEST IT OUT** **T**

# Plan of Action

You are unlikely to meet with much success if you launch into negotiation without thinking about what you hope to achieve. The plan outlined below aims to prevent this.

**1**

ESTABLISH the situation in your own mind – what you have to bargain with; how far you're willing to compromise; any result you would find unacceptable. Ensure that you know the facts.

**2**

DISCUSS the situation with the relevant party, each of you clarifying how you view the situation and voicing your respective needs.

**3**

PROPOSE a solution, generally involving a degree of compromise. Be open to suggestions – you may reach a compromise you hadn't envisaged but that satisfies you more than your original plan.

**4**

CONCLUDE the negotiation properly, having established what terms both parties have come to an agreement about. Be amicable – it doesn't take much to please others, and can reward you immensely in a tight corner.

# Remember: anything is possible if you want it that much.

Deciding what you want is half the battle – then all
you have to do is do it!

# General self-assessment quiz

**Your Score**

20-33 Good communication isn't really one of your strongest points. You may find it easy to talk to others, but have you really considered if your words of wisdom are appreciated? Continually focusing on yourself is unlikely to make a good impression. Or perhaps you find it hard to say anything at all, which can be just as bad: people may interpret this is as unfriendliness, rather than shyness. Relax, concentrate on being interested in others rather than worrying about yourself, and things will improve. You should try to be more willing to adapt to each situation: for example, you may create a more favourable impression by considering the dress, attitudes and conversation that fit a particular occasion.

34-47 Although you seem to make quite an effort where communication is concerned, you are prone to lapses that let you down. These may easily be corrected by a more thoughtful, considered approach – clarifying exactly what you want to get out of each situation may provide sufficient insight to help you achieve the results you deserve. Lack of confidence may be all that is holding back your communication skills.

48-60 Your shrewd ability to act according to the situation, gauging how to conduct yourself most appropriately, is very admirable. You appear to be aware of others, recognizing the need to listen in order to put your own thoughts across with the maximum effect. Your popularity stems from your willingness to approach others and be approached – you know that a friendly smile or gesture is just as effective as saying hello. Don't get complacent though – there are always new communication skills to learn.

# Would You or Wouldn't You?

**Scoring**

| | a. | b. | c. | | a. | b. | c. |
|---|---|---|---|---|---|---|---|
| 1. | 1 | 2 | 0 | 9. | 2 | 1 | 0 |
| 2. | 2 | 0 | 1 | 10. | 1 | 0 | 2 |
| 3. | 1 | 0 | 2 | 11. | 0 | 2 | 1 |
| 4. | 2 | 1 | 0 | 12. | 2 | 1 | 0 |
| 5. | 2 | 0 | 1 | 13. | 0 | 1 | 2 |
| 6. | 0 | 1 | 2 | 14. | 1 | 2 | 0 |
| 7. | 0 | 2 | 1 | 15. | 0 | 1 | 2 |
| 8. | 1 | 2 | 0 | | | | |

**Your Score**

0-10: Poor. But everyone can learn to communicate better.

11-20: Good, although acting with a little more sensitivity and confidence may be worthwhile.

21-30: Excellent. You seem to be sensitive to the unique communication skills required for each situation.

# INTRODUCTION TO LOGIC PUZZLES

People often feel that there's something a bit cold about logic. It reminds us of Mr Spock playing multidimensional chess, his mighty Vulcan brain remorselessly analysing every possible permutation of the game. Even worse, it makes us think of mathematics lessons where we sweated over some ghastly geometrical conundrum that stubbornly refused to yield up its dusty secrets. Fortunately it does not have to be that way.

Ken Russell and Philip Carter, who have for many years been Mensa's resident puzzle experts, have come up with a collection of logic problems just for fun. The nice thing about logic is that it does not require any special knowledge, just a capacity for following an argument one step at a time to its inevitable conclusion. There is something extremely satisfying in being able to take a knotty problem and, after having carefully unpicked the complications, arriving at the solution.

# Dazzling Diamond

Divide the diamond into four identical shapes, each containing one of each of the following five symbols:

see answer
21

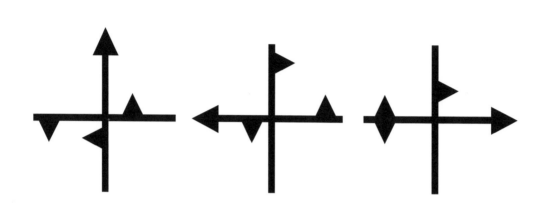

Look at the three shapes. Does option A, B, C, D or E continue the sequence?

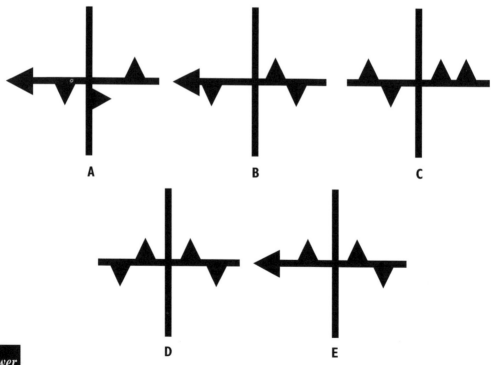

A

B

C

D

E

see answer
5

120

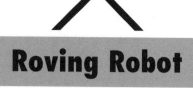

# Roving Robot

Scientists have produced a robot that contains a simple program
for crossing a quiet road (not a one-way street) in the UK.

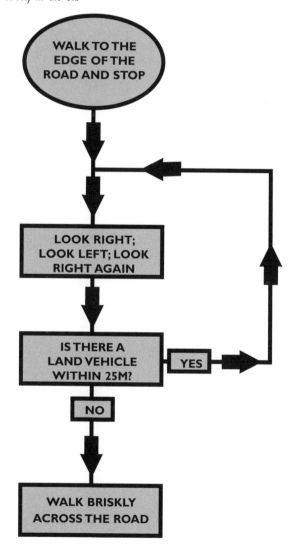

WALK TO THE
EDGE OF THE
ROAD AND STOP

LOOK RIGHT;
LOOK LEFT; LOOK
RIGHT AGAIN

IS THERE A
LAND VEHICLE
WITHIN 25M?

YES

NO

WALK BRISKLY
ACROSS THE ROAD

But they made a cardinal error and the robot takes eight hours
to cross the road. What is the error?

*see answer*

**20**

# Three Circles

Draw three complete circles so that each circle contains one ellipse, one square and one triangle.

see answer
**2**

# Counterfeit Coins

Most counterfeit coin puzzles assume you have balance-type scales available with two pans, where one object is weighed against another. In this puzzle you have a single scale with only one pan. You have three bags of large gold coins with an unspecified number of coins in each bag. One of the bags consists entirely of conterfeit coins weighing 55g each; the other two bags contain all genuine coins weighing 50g each.

What is the minimum number of weighing operations you need to carry out before you can be certain of identifying the bag of counterfeit coins?

*see answer*
**15**

# Sitting Pretty

At the school the boys sit at desks numbered 1–5 and the girls sit opposite them at desks numbered 6–10.

1. The girl sitting next to the girl opposite no. 1 is Fiona.
2. Fiona is three desks away from Grace.
3. Hilary is opposite Colin.
4. Eddy is opposite the girl next to Hilary.
5. If Colin is not central then Alan is.
6. David is next to Bill.
7. Bill is three desks away from Colin.
8. If Fiona is not central then Indira is.
9. Hilary is three desks away from Jane.
10. David is opposite Grace.
11. The girl sitting next to the girl opposite Alan is Jane.
12. Colin is not at desk no. 5.
13. Jane is not at desk no. 10.

Can you work out the seating arrangements?

*see answer*
**16**

# Making Eyes

Look at the five drawings. Does A, B, C, D or E continue the sequence?

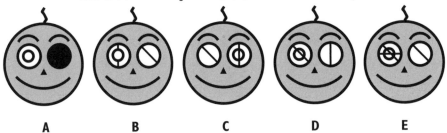

**see answer**
**13**

A    B    C    D    E

# Figure of Fun

Look at the five figures. Which of the following options continues the sequence?

A    B    C    D    E

**see answer**
**17**

# Converging Circles

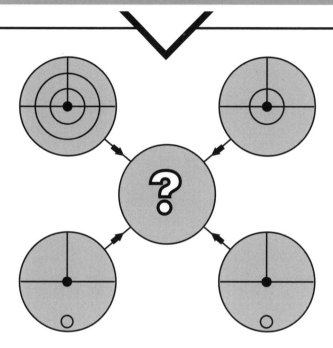

Each line and symbol in the four outer circles is transferred to the middle circle according to a few rules. These are that if a line or symbol occurs in the outer circles:

once, it is transferred; twice, it is possibly transferred; three times, it is transferred; four times, it is not transferred.

Which of the five circles should appear in the middle of the diagram above?

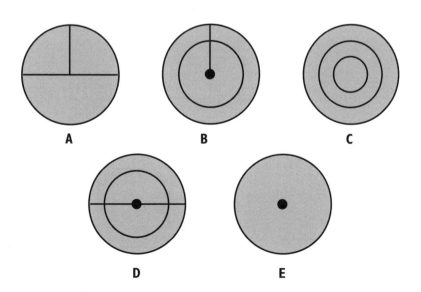

A        B        C

D        E

see answer
10

# Shooting Range

Three military marksmen — Colonel Present, Major Aim and General Fire — are shooting on the range. When they have finished, they collect their targets.

Each makes three statements:

Colonel Present:
"I scored 180."
"I scored 40 less than the major."
"I scored 20 more than the general."

Major Aim:
"I did not score the lowest."
"The difference between my score and the general's was 60."
"The general scored 240."

General Fire:
"I scored less than the colonel."
"The colonel scored 200."
"The major scored 60 more than the colonel."

see answer
14

Each marksman makes one incorrect statement. What are their scores?

# Land of Zoz

In the land of Zoz there live three types of person:

Truthkins, who live in hexagonal houses and always tell the truth;
Fibkins, who live in pentagonal houses and always tell lies;
Switchkins, who live in round houses and who make true whatever they say.

One morning 90 of them gather in the city in three groups of 30. One group is all of one type; another group is made up evenly of two types; the third group evenly comprises three types. Everyone in one group says "We are all truthkins"; everyone in a second group says "We are all fibkins"; and everyone in the third group says "We are all switchkins".

see answer
12

How many sleep in pentagonal houses that night?

# Fancy Figures

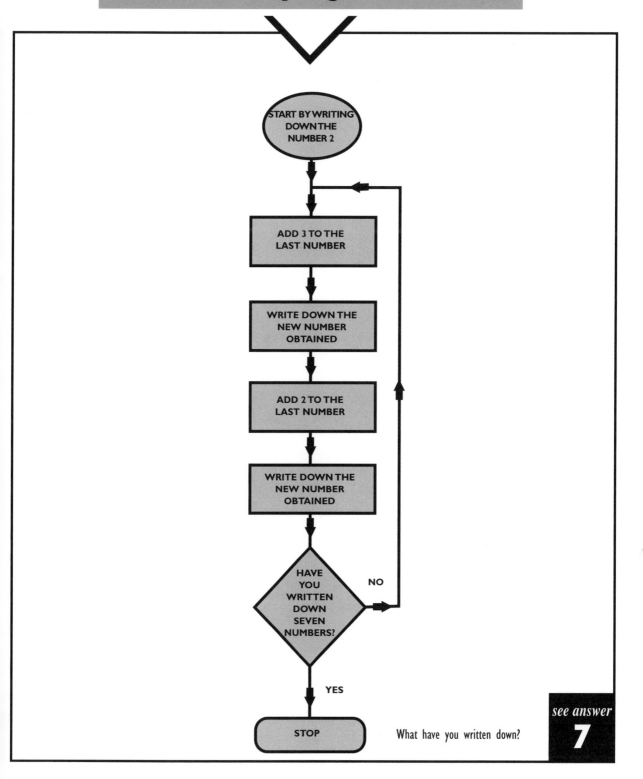

START BY WRITING DOWN THE NUMBER 2

ADD 3 TO THE LAST NUMBER

WRITE DOWN THE NEW NUMBER OBTAINED

ADD 2 TO THE LAST NUMBER

WRITE DOWN THE NEW NUMBER OBTAINED

HAVE YOU WRITTEN DOWN SEVEN NUMBERS?

NO

YES

STOP

What have you written down?

*see answer*
**7**

127

The new repairer starts work repairing telephones. There are 15 booths in his area. The supervisor tells him that five out of the first eight booths need repairing and that he should go and repair one as a test.

The man goes straight to booth number eight. Why?

see answer

4

# Hexagon Harmony

Look at the three hexagons. Which of the following four options continues the sequence?

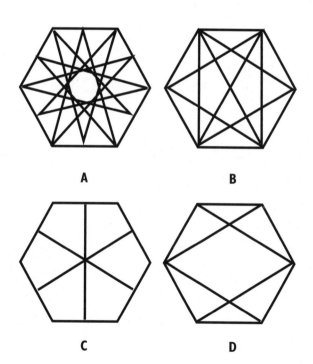

A          B

C          D

see answer
8

# Las Vegas

Three gamblers — Diablo, Scarface and Lucky — attend a convention at Las Vegas. They decide to have a gambling session with six-sided dice, but stipulate unusual rules:

1. Each gambler may select his own numbers.
2. The numbers 1–9 may be selected, but no two numbers may be consecutive.
3. Each die has to have three pairs of different numbers, adding up to 30.

In addition, no two gamblers are allowed to choose the same combination of numbers. In a long run, Diablo's numbers will beat Scarface; Scarface's numbers will beat Lucky; but Lucky's numbers will beat Diablo. How is this possible?

see answer
**1**

# Murder in Mind

Four suspects — Jack Vicious, Sid Shifty, Alf Muggins and Jim Pouncer — are being interviewed at the scene of a murder. Each of the suspects is asked a question. Their answers are as follows:

Jack Vicious: "Sid Shifty committed the murder."
Sid Shifty: "Jim Pouncer committed the murder."
Alf Muggins: "I didn't commit the murder."
Jim Pouncer: "Sid Shifty is lying."

Only one of the four answers is the truth. Who committed the murder?

see answer
**6**

# Dynamic Dog

Russell Carter lives on a remote ranch in the Australian outback with his dog, Spot. Several times a week he sets off with Spot for a long walk. This morning he is walking at a steady 4mph and when they are 10 miles from home he turns to go home and, retracing his steps, lets Spot off the lead. Spot immediately runs homeward at 9mph. When Spot reaches the ranch he turns around and runs back to Russell, who is continuing at his steady 4mph. On reaching Russell, Spot turns back for the ranch, maintaining his 9mph. This is repeated until Russell arrives back at the ranch and lets Spot in. At all times Russell and Spot maintain their respective speeds of 4mph and 9mph.

How many miles does Spot cover from being let off the lead to being let into the ranch?

see answer
19

# Manor House

In the English countryside is a traditional manor house. Five staff work there, each of whom has a different hobby and a different rest day.

1. The man who has Tuesday off plays golf but is not the janitor, who is called Clark.
2. Jones is not the butler who plays squash.
3. Wood has Wednesday off and is not the butler or the gardener.
4. James is the cook and does not have Thursdays off; Smith also does not have Thursdays off.
5. Bridge is played on Monday; the chauffeur does not play chess; and James does not have Tuesdays off.

What are their names, how is each employed, what is the pastime of each, and on which day of the week does each have a rest day?

| | | OCCUPATION | | | | | PASTIME | | | | | DAY | | | | |
|---|---|---|---|---|---|---|---|---|---|---|---|---|---|---|---|---|
| | | BUTLER | CHAUFFEUR | COOK | GARDENER | JANITOR | FISHING | CHESS | SQUASH | BRIDGE | GOLF | MONDAY | TUESDAY | WEDNESDAY | THURSDAY | FRIDAY |
| **NAME** | SMITH | | | | | | | | | | | | | | | |
| | JONES | | | | | | | | | | | | | | | |
| | WOOD | | | | | | | | | | | | | | | |
| | CLARK | | | | | | | | | | | | | | | |
| | JAMES | | | | | | | | | | | | | | | |
| **DAY** | MONDAY | | | | | | | | | | | | | | | |
| | TUESDAY | | | | | | | | | | | | | | | |
| | WEDNESDAY | | | | | | | | | | | | | | | |
| | THURSDAY | | | | | | | | | | | | | | | |
| | FRIDAY | | | | | | | | | | | | | | | |
| **PASTIME** | FISHING | | | | | | | | | | | | | | | |
| | CHESS | | | | | | | | | | | | | | | |
| | SQUASH | | | | | | | | | | | | | | | |
| | BRIDGE | | | | | | | | | | | | | | | |
| | GOLF | | | | | | | | | | | | | | | |

| NAME | OCCUPATION | PASTIME | REST |
|---|---|---|---|
| | | | |
| | | | |
| | | | |
| | | | |
| | | | |

see answer
9

# House Hunting

My friend Archibald has moved into a new house in a long road in which the houses are numbered consecutively, 1–82. To find out his house number I ask him three questions to which I receive a yes/no answer. I will not tell you the answers, but if you can work them out you will discover his house number. The questions are:

1. Is it under 41?
2. Is it divisible by 4?
3. Is it a square number?

Can you work out the number of Archibald's house?

*see answer*
**18**

# Town Clock

From my window I can see the town clock. Every day I check the clock on my mantlepiece against the time shown on the town clock. It usually agrees; but one morning a strange situation occurred: on my mantlepiece stands my clock and it showed the time as 5 minutes to 9 o'clock; 1 minute later it read 4 minutes to 9 o'clock; 2 minutes later it read 4 minutes to 9 o'clock; 1 minute later it read 5 minutes to 9 o'clock.

At 9 o'clock I suddenly realized what was wrong. Can you tell what it was?

*see answer*
**3**

# Sears Tower

The former national headquarters of Sears Roebuck & Co. in Chicago, Illinois, was once the tallest inhabited building in the world. Better known as Sears Tower, it is 221m high plus half its height again.

How high is Sears Tower?

*see answer*
**11**

## Japan Hotel

In a hotel in Nagasaki is a glass door. On the door it says:

What does it mean?

see answer
**22**

## Prisoners' Porridge

A jailer has a large number of prisoners to guard and has to seat them at a number of tables at mealtimes. The regulations state the following seating arrangements:

1. Each table is to seat the same number of prisoners.
2. The number at each table is to be an odd number.

The jailer finds that when he seats the prisoners:
3 per table, he has 2 prisoners left over;
5 per table, he has 4 prisoners left over;
7 per table, he has 6 prisoners left over;
9 per table, he has 8 prisoners left over;
but when he seats them 11 per table there are none left over.

What is the least number of prisoners there can be?

see answer
**34**

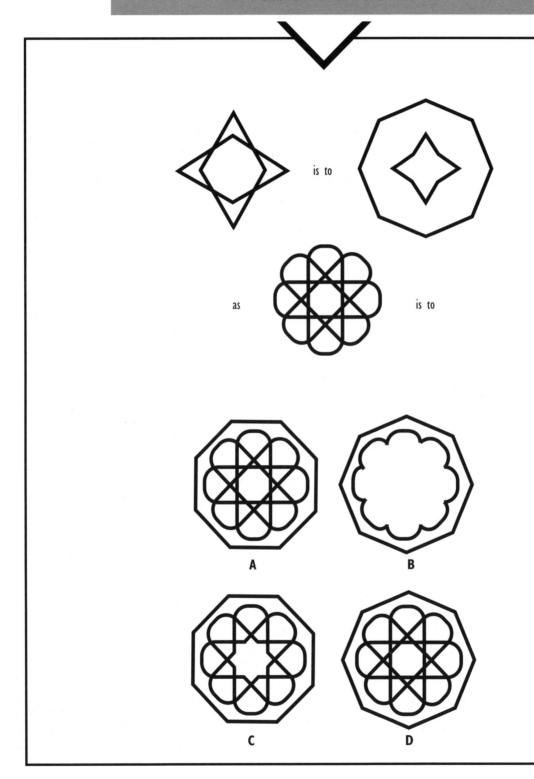

is to

as

is to

A

B

C

D

see answer
25

# Algarve Rendezvous

On the far eastern side of the Algarve, close to the Spanish border, is a town whose roads are laid out in grid fashion, like Manhattan. This system was first used in the cities of Ancient Greece. Seven friends live at different corners, marked  . They wish to meet for coffee.

On which corner should they meet in order to minimize the walking distance for all seven?

see answer
**31**

# Intergalactic Ingenuity

Five pairs of husband and wife aliens arrive for the intergalactic meeting on Earth. For ease of recognition, the males are known by the letter M followed by an odd number and the females by F and an even number. Each pair has different distinguishing features and has prepared a different subject for discussion. They arrive in different types of spacecraft and dock in a set of five bays. The pairs sit in five double seats in the auditorium.

1. M1 is preparing his speech on time travel and has arrived in a warp distorter.

2. The mind-reading couple who have four arms each have parked their nebula accelerator between the space oscillator and the astro carrier.

3. F6, in the seat next to the left-end pair, says to the alien next to her, "My husband M3 and I have noticed that you have three legs."

4. F4 admires the galaxy freighter owned by the pair who each have three eyes, who are in the next seats.

5. The husband of F8 is turning his papers on time travel with 12 fingers.

6. M5, in the middle pair of seats, says to F10 in the next pair of seats, "The pair with webbed feet on your other side have an astro carrier."

7. M7 and F2 are studying their papers on anti-gravity. The husband of F6 is studying his papers on nuclear fission.

| | FEMALE | | | | FEATURES | | | | | VEHICLE | | | | | SPEECH | | | | |
| --- | F2 | F4 | F6 | F8 | F10 | 3 EYES | 3 LEGS | 4 ARMS | 12 FINGERS | WEBBED FEET | ASTRO CARRIER | GALAXY FREIGHTER | NEBULA ACCELERATOR | SPACE OSCILLATOR | WARP DISTORTER | ANTI-GRAVITY | ASTRAL TRANSPORTING | MIND READING | NUCLEAR FISSION | TIME TRAVEL |
| **MALE** M1 | | | | | | | | | | | | | | | | | | | | |
| M3 | | | | | | | | | | | | | | | | | | | | |
| M5 | | | | | | | | | | | | | | | | | | | | |
| M7 | | | | | | | | | | | | | | | | | | | | |
| M9 | | | | | | | | | | | | | | | | | | | | |
| **SPEECH** ANTI-GRAVITY | | | | | | | | | | | | | | | | | | | | |
| ASTRAL TRANSPORTING | | | | | | | | | | | | | | | | | | | | |
| MIND READING | | | | | | | | | | | | | | | | | | | | |
| NUCLEAR FISSION | | | | | | | | | | | | | | | | | | | | |
| TIME TRAVEL | | | | | | | | | | | | | | | | | | | | |
| **VEHICLE** ASTRO | | | | | | | | | | | | | | | | | | | | |
| CARRIER | | | | | | | | | | | | | | | | | | | | |
| GALAXY FREIGHTER | | | | | | | | | | | | | | | | | | | | |
| NEBULA ACCELERATOR | | | | | | | | | | | | | | | | | | | | |
| SPACE OSCILLATOR | | | | | | | | | | | | | | | | | | | | |
| **FEATURES** WARP DISTORTER | | | | | | | | | | | | | | | | | | | | |
| 3 EYES | | | | | | | | | | | | | | | | | | | | |
| 3 LEGS | | | | | | | | | | | | | | | | | | | | |
| 4 ARMS | | | | | | | | | | | | | | | | | | | | |
| 12 FINGERS | | | | | | | | | | | | | | | | | | | | |

Who is the wife of M9 and who is the male speaker on nuclear fission?

see answer
**29**

| MALE/FEMALE | | | | | |
| --- | --- | --- | --- | --- | --- |
| SPEECH | | | | | |
| VEHICLE | | | | | |
| FEATURES | | | | | |

# Creative Circles

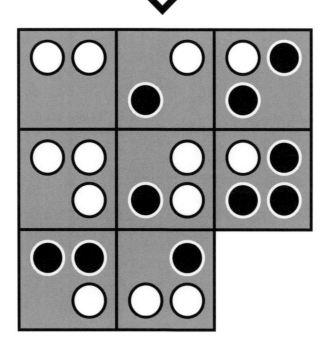

Look along each line and down each column of this shape. Which of the following eight options is the missing square?

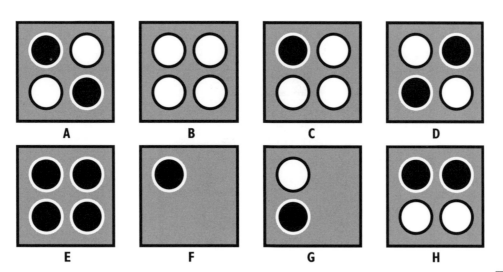

A    B    C    D

E    F    G    H

see answer
**35**

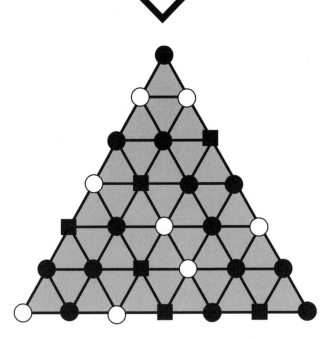

Place the 12 segment links below over the triangular grid in such a way that each link symbol on the grid is covered by an identical symbol. The connecting segments must not be rotated. Not all the connecting lines will be covered.

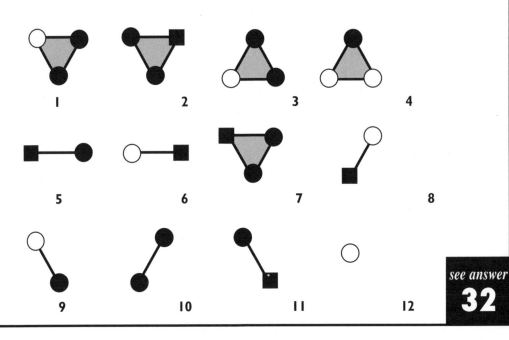

see answer
**32**

140

# Funny Fingers

There is a number of aliens in a room, more than one. Each alien has more than one finger on each hand. All aliens have the same number of fingers as each other. All aliens have a different number of fingers on each hand. If you knew the total number of fingers in the room you would know how many aliens were in the room. There are between 200 and 300 alien fingers in the room.

How many aliens are in the room?

see answer
**24**

# Think of a Number

Anastasia has thought of a number between 99 and 999. Belinda asks whether the number is below 500; Anastasia answers yes. Belinda asks whether the number is a square number; Anastasia answers yes. Belinda asks whether the number is a cube number; Anastasia answers yes. However, Anastasia has told the truth to only two of the three questions. Anastasia then tells Belinda truthfully that both the first and the last digit are 5, 7 or 9.

What is the number?

see answer
**36**

| 5 | ? | 5 7 9 |
|---|---|-------|
| 7 | ? | 5 7 9 |
| 9 | ? | 5 7 9 |

# Girl Talk

A census-taker calls at a house. He asks the woman living there the ages of her three daughters.

The woman says, "If you multiply their ages the total is 72; if you add together their ages the total is the same as the number on my front door, which you can see."

The census-taker says, "That is not enough information for me to calculate their ages."

The woman says, "Well, my eldest daughter has a cat with a wooden leg."

The census-taker replies, "Ah! Now I know their ages."

What are the ages of the three girls?

see answer
**42**

# Treasured Trees

Local sports clubs take turns to plant a tree each year in the town's main street. A bird has established a nest in each tree.

1. The crow lives in the beech tree.
2. The lime was planted two years after the tree planted by the golf club.
3. The robin is in the tree planted by the bowling club, which is next to the tree planted by the soccer club.
4. Jim planted his tree in 1971.
5. The starling is in the poplar tree planted by Desmond in 1974.
6. The robin lives in the tree planted by the bowling club, which is next to the tree planted by the soccer club.
7. Tony planted the middle tree — a beech.
8. Bill has an owl in his tree, which is next to the ash.
9. The tree at the right-hand end was planted in 1974 by the soccer club.
10. The elm was planted in 1970.
11. The tennis club planted in 1972.
12. The squash club planted in 1970.
13. Sylvester planted his tree in 1973 and it has a robin in it.
14. The blackbird is in the tree planted by Jim.

Work out which tree was planted by which member of each club and in which year.

| | | | | | |
|---|---|---|---|---|---|
| **TREE** | | | | | |
| **PERSON** | | | | | |
| **CLUB** | | | | | |
| **BIRD** | | | | | |
| **YEAR** | | | | | |

*see answer*
## 28

# Club Conundrum

There are 189 members of the tennis club: 8 have been at the club less than three years; 11 are under 20 years of age; 70 wear spectacles; 140 are men.

What is the smallest number of players who had been members for three years or more, were at least 20 years of age, wore glasses and were men?

see answer
**38**

# Tree Teaser

Don and Spencer are engaged by the local council to prune trees on either side of a tree-lined avenue. There is an equal number of trees on either side of the road. Don arrives first and has pruned three trees on the right-hand side when Spencer arrives and points out that Don should be pruning the trees on the left-hand side. So Don starts afresh on the left-hand side and Spencer continues on the right. When Spencer has finished his side he goes across the avenue and prunes six trees for Don, which finishes the job.

Who prunes the most trees and by how many?

see answer
**41**

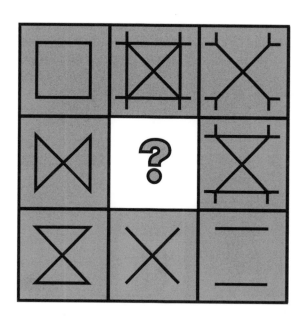

Look at the pattern of tiles. Which of the following tiles replaces the question mark?

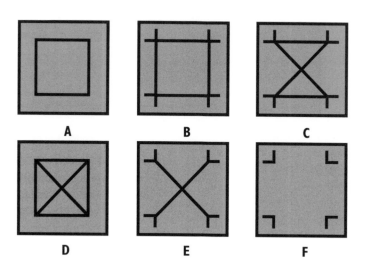

A    B    C

D    E    F

see answer
33

# Dog Delight

There is a somewhat confusing situation at the dog show this year. Four brothers — Andy, Bill, Colin and Donald — each enter two dogs, and each has named his dogs after two of his brothers. Consequently, there are two dogs named Andy, two named Bill, two named Colin and two named Donald.

Of the eight dogs, three are corgis, three labradors and two dalmatians. None of the four brothers owns two dogs of the same breed. No two dogs of the same breed have the same name. Neither of Andy's dogs is named Donald and neither of Colin's dogs is named Andy. No corgi is named Andy and no labrador is named Donald. Bill does not own a labrador.

Who are the owners of the dalmatians and what are the dalmatians' names?

*see answer*
**37**

# Handkerchief Challenge

Charlie throws out a challenge to Ben in the local bar: "I'll put this ordinary pocket handkerchief on the floor. You stand on one corner and I'll stand on the other corner. Without either of us tearing, cutting, stretching or altering it in any way, I bet you won't be able to touch me."

How can this be done?

*see answer*
**30**

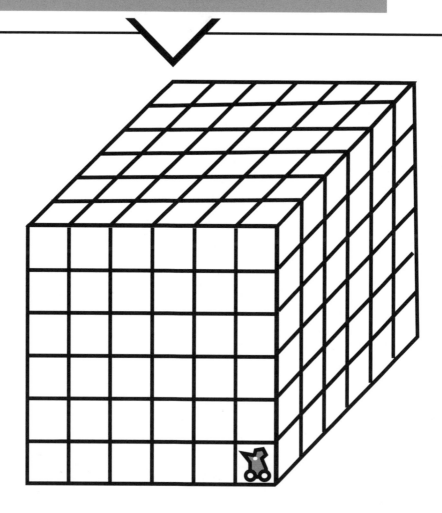

The cage consists of 216 open chambers. An electronic robot mouse is placed in the bottom right-hand front chamber, marked above. You are able to operate the mouse by remote control, moving it three chambers to the right or left and two chambers up or down.

Are you able to get the mouse into the central chamber, and if so, what is the minimum number of moves by which this can be achieved?

*see answer*
**27**

# Roulette Riddle

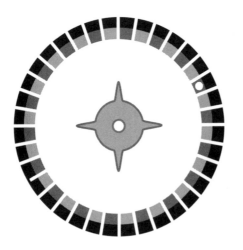

A roulette wheel shows the numbers 1–36. My ball has landed on a particular number. It is divisible by 3. When the digits are added together, the total lies between 4 and 8. It is an odd number. When the digits are multiplied together the total lies between 4 and 8.

Which number have I bet on?

see answer
**40**

# Salary Increase

A company gives a choice of two plans to the union negotiator for an increase in salary. The first option is an initial salary of $20,000 to be increased after 12 months by $500. The second option is an initial salary of $20,000 to be increased after each six months by $125. The salary is to be calculated every six months.

Can you advise the union negotiator which is the plan he should recommend to his members?

see answer
**23**

# Three Squares

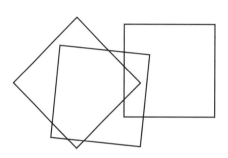

Look at the group of three squares. They have a certain feature which is shared by only one of the groups of three squares below. What is it, and which group matches?

**A**

**B**

**C**

**D**

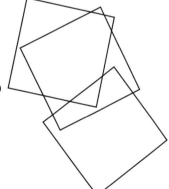

see answer
**39**

# Barrels of Fun

A wine merchant has six barrels of wine and beer containing
30 gallons
32 gallons
36 gallons
38 gallons
40 gallons
62 gallons

Five barrels are filled with wine and one with beer.
The first customer purchases two barrels of wine; the second customer purchases twice as much wine as the first customer.

Which barrel contains beer?

see answer
26

# Table Talk

Four women are seated around a table. Where should you be seated in order to be the greatest distance from all four women measured around the edge of the table?

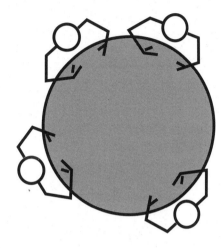

see answer
58

# Number Placement

| | 14 | 10 | 7 |
|---|---|---|---|
| 9 | 6 | | 4 |
| 16 | | 13 | 11 |
| 12 | 8 | 5 | 15 |

The numbers 4–16 have already been inserted into the grid, almost — but not quite — at random. Following just two simple rules, where would you place the numbers 1, 2 and 3 in the grid?

see answer
44

# Study Time

Three college students — Anne, Bess and Candice — each study four subjects. Two of them study physics; two study algebra; two study English; two study history; two study French; two study Japanese.

Anne:  if she studies algebra then she also takes history;
       if she studies history she does not take English;
       if she studies English she does not take Japanese.

Bess:  if she studies English she also takes Japanese;
       if she studies Japanese she does not take algebra;
       if she studies algebra she does not take French.

Candice:  if she studies French she does not take algebra;
          if she does not study algebra she studies Japanese;
          if she studies Japanese she does not take English.

What do you know about these three students?

|  | ANNE | BESS | CANDICE |
|---|---|---|---|
| PHYSICS |  |  |  |
| ALGEBRA |  |  |  |
| ENGLISH |  |  |  |
| HISTORY |  |  |  |
| FRENCH |  |  |  |
| JAPANESE |  |  |  |

see answer
47

# Picking Professions

Mr Carter, Mr Butler, Mr Drover and Mr Hunter are employed as a carter, a butler, a drover and a hunter. None of them has a name identifying their profession. They made four statements:

I. Mr Carter is the hunter.    2. Mr Drover is the carter.    3. Mr Butler is not the hunter.    4. Mr Hunter is not the butler.

According to those statements, the butler must be Mr Butler, but this cannot be correct. Three of the four statements are untrue. Who is the drover?

see answer
49

# Gone Fishing

Five men staying at the coastal hotel decide to go fishing on the pier. They sit next to each other, using different bait, and catch different numbers of fish.

1. The plumber, called Henry, catches one fish fewer than Dick.
2. The electrician is next to the banker and uses bread for his bait.
3. The man at the north end of the pier is the banker, who is sitting next to Fred.
4. The salesman catches only one fish, and is sitting at the south end of the pier.
5. Meal is the bait used by Malcolm, and the man from Orlando catches 15 fish.
6. The man from New York uses shrimps for bait and is sitting next to the man who catches one fish.
7. Joe is from Los Angeles and uses worms as his bait.
8. The man in the middle is from Tucson and uses a bait of maggots.
9. The banker catches six fish.
10. Dick, who is the middle fisherman, is two seats away from the man from St Louis.
11. The man who is sitting next to the man from New York catches 10 fish and is a professor.
12. Henry did not sit next to Joe.

Work out where each man lives, his occupation, the bait he is using, and how many fish he catches.

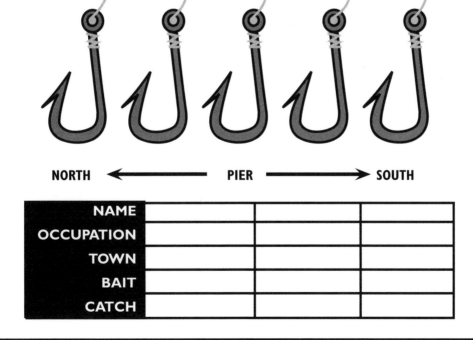

NORTH ← PIER → SOUTH

| NAME | | | |
|---|---|---|---|
| OCCUPATION | | | |
| TOWN | | | |
| BAIT | | | |
| CATCH | | | |

see answer
54

## Great Golfers

Mr Peters, Mr Edwards and Mr Roberts are playing a round of golf together. Half-way through the game Mr Peters remarks that he has just noticed that their first names are Peter, Edward and Robert. "Yes," says one of the others, "I'd noticed that too, but none of us has the same surname as our own first name. For example, my first name is Robert."

What are the full names of the three golfers?

*see answer*
**50**

## Best Beer

A man can drink a barrel of beer in 27 days.
A woman can drink a barrel of beer in 54 days.

If they both drink out of the same barrel at their respective rates, how long will it take for the barrel to be emptied?

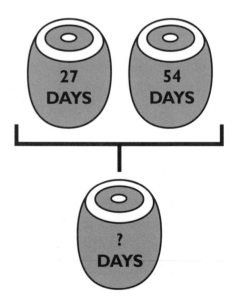

*see answer*
**63**

# Pleased Pupils

There are five pupils, each in a different class. Each pupil takes a subject and sport which she enjoys.

1. The girl who plays squash likes algebra and is not in class 5.
2. Doris is in class 3 and Betty likes running.
3. The girl who likes running is in class 2.
4. The girl in class 4 likes swimming, and Elizabeth likes chemistry.
5. Alice is in class 6 and likes squash but not geography.
6. The girl who likes chemistry also enjoys basketball.
7. The girl who likes biology also likes running.
8. Clara likes history but not tennis.

Work out the class, subject and sport of each girl.

| | CLASS | | | | | SUBJECT | | | | | SPORT | | | | |
| | 2 | 3 | 4 | 5 | 6 | HISTORY | ALGEBRA | CHEMISTRY | GEOGRAPHY | BIOLOGY | TENNIS | SQUASH | SWIMMING | RUNNING | BASKETBALL |
| **NAME** ALICE | | | | | | | | | | | | | | | |
| BETT | | | | | | | | | | | | | | | |
| CLARA | | | | | | | | | | | | | | | |
| DORIS | | | | | | | | | | | | | | | |
| ELIZABETH | | | | | | | | | | | | | | | |
| **SPORT** TENNIS | | | | | | | | | | | | | | | |
| SQUASH | | | | | | | | | | | | | | | |
| SWIMMING | | | | | | | | | | | | | | | |
| RUNNING | | | | | | | | | | | | | | | |
| BASKETBALL | | | | | | | | | | | | | | | |
| **SUBJECT** HISTORY | | | | | | | | | | | | | | | |
| ALGEBRA | | | | | | | | | | | | | | | |
| CHEMISTRY | | | | | | | | | | | | | | | |
| GEOGRAPHY | | | | | | | | | | | | | | | |
| BIOLOGY | | | | | | | | | | | | | | | |

| NAME | CLASS | SUBJECT | SPORT |
|------|-------|---------|-------|
| | | | |
| | | | |
| | | | |
| | | | |
| | | | |

*see answer*

**52**

# Winning Wager

Bill says to Jim, "Let's have a wager on each frame. We will play for half of the money in your wallet on each frame, and we will have 10 frames. Since you have $8 in you wallet, we will play for $4 on the first frame. I will give you $4 if you win and you will give me $4 if I win. When we start the second frame you will have either $12 or $4, so we will play for $6 or $2, etc."

They play 10 frames. Bill wins four and loses six frames but Jim finds that he has only $5.70 left and so has lost $2.30. How is this possible?

see answer
**55**

# Cube Diagonals

Two diagonals have been drawn on two faces of the cube. Using logical reasoning and lateral thinking, can you work out the angle between the two diagonals AB and AC?

see answer
**62**

A clock on the wall falls to the floor and the face breaks into three pieces. The digits on each piece of clock add up to the same total. What are the digits on each piece?

*see answer*
**51**

# Changing Trains

A woman usually leaves work at 5.30pm, calls at the supermarket, then catches the 6pm train, which arrives at the station in her home town at 6.30pm. Her husband leaves home each day, drives to the station and picks her up at 6.30pm, just as she gets off the train.

Today the woman finishes work about five minutes earlier than usual, decides to go straight to the station instead of calling at the supermarket, and manages to catch the 5.30pm train, which arrives at her home station at 6pm. Since her husband is not there to pick her up she begins to walk home. Her husband leaves home at the usual time, sees his wife walking, turns around, picks her up and drives home, arriving there 10 minutes earlier than usual.

Assume that all the trains arrive precisely on time. For how long does the woman walk before her husband picks her up?

*see answer*
**59**

# Spot the Shape

Each of the nine squares in the grid marked 1A to 3C should incorporate all the lines and symbols which are shown in the squares of the same letter and number immediately above and to the left. For example, 2B should incorporate all the lines and symbols that are in 2 and B.

One of the squares is incorrect. Which is it?

see answer
57

# Fathers and Daughters

A group of friends get together with their daughters for the evening.

1. John is 52 years old and his daughter is not called Eve.
2. Len has a daughter aged 21 years, and Betty is three years older than Eve.
3. Kevin is 53 years old and Diana is 19 years old.
4. Eve is 18 years old, and Nick has a daughter called Carol.
5. Alison is 20 years old and her father is called John.
6. Kevin has a daughter aged 19 years, and Eve's father is called Malcolm.
7. Malcolm is three years older than Nick.

| | | FATHER'S AGE | | | | | DAUGHTER'S AGE | | | | | DAUGHTER | | | | |
| --- | --- | --- | --- | --- | --- | --- | --- | --- | --- | --- | --- | --- | --- | --- | --- | --- |
| | | 50 | 51 | 52 | 53 | 54 | 17 | 18 | 19 | 20 | 21 | ALISON | BETTY | CAROL | DIANA | EVE |
| FATHER | JOHN | | | | | | | | | | | | | | | |
| | KEVIN | | | | | | | | | | | | | | | |
| | LEN | | | | | | | | | | | | | | | |
| | MALCOLM | | | | | | | | | | | | | | | |
| | NICK | | | | | | | | | | | | | | | |
| DAUGHTER | ALISON | | | | | | | | | | | | | | | |
| | BETTY | | | | | | | | | | | | | | | |
| | CAROL | | | | | | | | | | | | | | | |
| | DIANA | | | | | | | | | | | | | | | |
| | EVE | | | | | | | | | | | | | | | |
| DAUGHTER'S AGE | 17 | | | | | | | | | | | | | | | |
| | 18 | | | | | | | | | | | | | | | |
| | 19 | | | | | | | | | | | | | | | |
| | 20 | | | | | | | | | | | | | | | |
| | 21 | | | | | | | | | | | | | | | |

| FATHER | DAUGHTER | FATHER'S AGE | DAUGHTER'S AGE |
| --- | --- | --- | --- |
| | | | |
| | | | |
| | | | |
| | | | |
| | | | |

see answer 60

# Sums about Sons

A woman has two sons, Graham and Frederick. Frederick is three times as old as Graham. If you square Frederick's age you arrive at the same total as when you cube Graham's age. If you subtract Graham's age from Frederick's you arrive at the number of steps in the path to the family's front door. If you add Graham's age to Frederick's you arrive at the number of palisades in the family's fence. If you multiply their ages you arrive at the number of bricks in the family's front wall.

If you add these last three numbers together you have the family's house number, which is 297.

How old are Graham and Frederick?

see answer
61

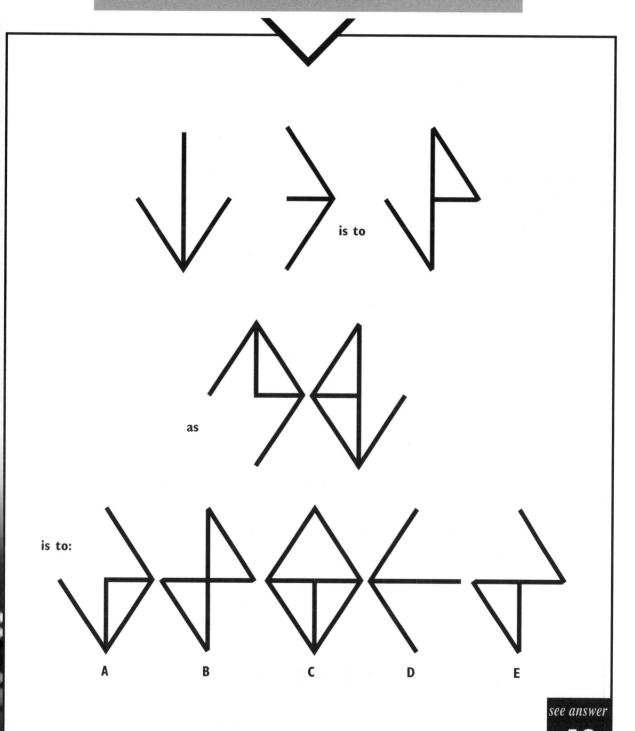

is to

as

is to:

A     B     C     D     E

see answer
43

# Play Watching

Four husband and wife couples go to see a play. They all sit in the same row, but no husband sits next to his wife, and a man and a woman are at opposite ends of the row. Their names are Andrews, Barker, Collins and Dunlop.

1. Mrs Dunlop or Mr Andrews is in the end seat.
2. Mr Andrews is mid-way between Mr Collins and Mrs Collins.
3. Mr Collins is two seats from Mrs Dunlop.
4. Mrs Collins is mid-way between Mr and Mrs Barker.
5. Mrs Andrews is next to the end seat.
6. Mr Dunlop is two seats from Mr Andrews.
7. Mrs Collins is closer to the right end than the left end.

Work out the seating arrangements along the row.

Feed information into the seats

see answer
**45**

# Trying Triangles

What is the smallest number of segments of equal area and
shape that the rectangle can be divided into so that each
segment contains the same number of triangles?

see answer
**48**

# Hello Sailor

Five sailors of different rank are at different ports on different ships.

1. Manning is at the Falklands, and the purser is Dewhurst.
2. Brand is on a warship, and the purser is not on the cruiser.
3. Perkins is on the aircraft carrier, and Ward is at Portsmouth.
4. The commander is at the Falklands, and Manning is on a submarine.
5. The warship is at Crete, and Perkins is at Malta.
6. The frigate is at Gibraltar and the steward is at Malta.
7. Brand is a captain and the seaman is not on the frigate.

Work out the details of each sailor.

| | RANK | | | | | SHIP | | | | | LOCATION | | | | |
|---|---|---|---|---|---|---|---|---|---|---|---|---|---|---|---|
| | COMMANDER | CAPTAIN | STEWARD | PURSER | SEAMAN | CRUISER | WARSHIP | FRIGATE | SUBMARINE | AIRCRAFT CARRIER | MALTA | CRETE | FALKLANDS | GIBRALTAR | PORTSMOUTH |
| **PERKINS** | | | | | | | | | | | | | | | |
| **WARD** | | | | | | | | | | | | | | | |
| **MANNING** | | | | | | | | | | | | | | | |
| **DEWHURST** | | | | | | | | | | | | | | | |
| **BRAND** | | | | | | | | | | | | | | | |
| **MALTA** | | | | | | | | | | | | | | | |
| **CRETE** | | | | | | | | | | | | | | | |
| **FALKLANDS** | | | | | | | | | | | | | | | |
| **GIBRALTAR** | | | | | | | | | | | | | | | |
| **PORTSMOUTH** | | | | | | | | | | | | | | | |
| **CRUISER** | | | | | | | | | | | | | | | |
| **WARSHIP** | | | | | | | | | | | | | | | |
| **FRIGATE** | | | | | | | | | | | | | | | |
| **SUBMARINE** | | | | | | | | | | | | | | | |
| **AIRCRAFT CARRIER** | | | | | | | | | | | | | | | |

NAME — LOCATION — SHIP

| NAME | RANK | SHIP | LOCATION |
|---|---|---|---|
| | | | |
| | | | |
| | | | |
| | | | |
| | | | |

*see answer*
**53**

164

# Suspicious Circles

Which of these circles is the odd one out?

A

B

C

D

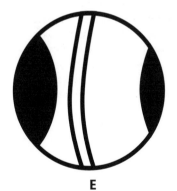

E

see answer
46

Which of the following six shapes is the odd one out?

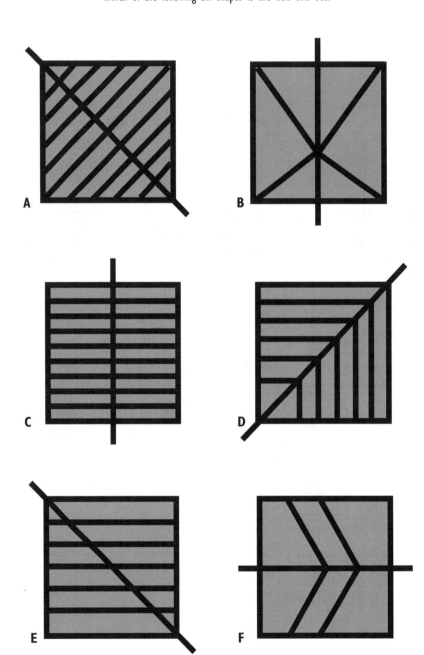

see answer
**56**

# Broadway, NY

In Broadway, New York City, a man sees one of those new-fangled buses. It was stationary and he could not tell which way it was going.

Can you?

*see answer*
**74**

A ⟷     B ⟷

# Logical Clocks

These clocks follow a weird kind of logic. What time should the fourth clock show? Choose from the four options provided.

A     B     C     D

*see answer*
**73**

# Round and Round the Garden

A woman has a garden path 2m wide, with a hedge on either side. The path spirals into the middle of the garden. One day the woman walks the length of the path, finishing in the middle. Ignore the width of the hedge and assume she walks in the middle of the path. How far does she walk?

see answer
**80**

# Rifle Range

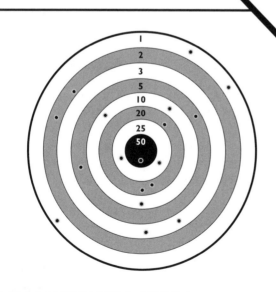

Three soldiers — Colonel Ketchup, Major Mustard and Captain Chutney — have a shooting competition. They each fire six shots and each score 71 points. Colonel Ketchup's first two shots score 22; Major Mustard's first shot scores 3.

Who hits the bull's eye?

see answer
**67**

# Missing Links

| 74882 | 3584 | |

| 29637 | | 192 |

| 74826 | | |

Fill in the missing numbers from these bars. Just enough information has been provided to work out the logic. The logic is the same in each line of numbers.

Now try this one:

| 528 | 116 | |

| 793 | | 335 |

| 821 | | |

see answer
76

# Gun Running

Bully Bill and Dynamo Dan are cattle ranchers. One day they decide to sell their stock and become sheep farmers. They take the cattle to market and receive for each steer a number of dollars equal to the total number of steer that they sell. With this money they purchase sheep at $10 per head, and with the money left over they purchase a goat.

On the way home they argue and so decide to divide up their stock, but find that they have one sheep over. So Bully Bill keeps the sheep and gives Dynamo Dan the goat.

"But I have less than you," says Dynamo Dan, "because a goat is worth less than a sheep."

"Alright," says Bully Bill, "I will give you my Colt .45 to make up the difference."

What is the value of the Colt .45?

see answer
65

# Black and White Balls

see answer
**70**

This probability problem can be solved through logical thought.

You have two bags, each one containing eight balls: four white and four black. A ball is drawn out of bag one and another ball out of bag two.

What are the chances that at least one of the balls is black?

**BAG ONE**          **BAG TWO**

# Triangles and Trapeziums

is to

as

is to

A     B     C     D

see answer
**83**

# Dice Dilemma

Here are views of six non-standard, six-sided dice. Which of the six dice cannot be made up from the following?

1    2    3    4    5    6    NET

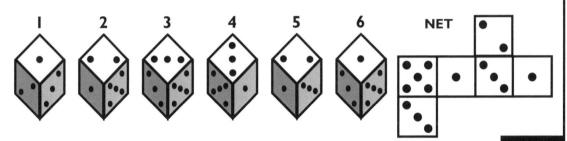

see answer
**82**

# Carrier Pigeons

A driver approaches a bridge. He notices that the maximum weight allowed is 20 tons and knows that his empty pantechnicon weighs 20 tons. However, he has a cargo of 200 pigeons which weigh 1lb each. As the pigeons are asleep on perches he stops the vehicle, bangs on the side to waken the birds who start flying around, then safely drives over the bridge.

Is he correct?

BRIDGE
MAX. WEIGHT
20 TONS

HOMING
PIGEONS

see answer
**71**

# Circles and Triangles

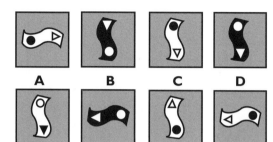

Look along each line and down each column and work out which is the missing square from these options:

see answer
**64**

# City Slicker

City blocks have been built between two main roads —A and B — in a grid, like Manhattan, New York. Always moving toward B, how many different routes are there?

see answer
**77**

# Missing Numbers

There is a logic behind the distribution of numbers in the grid. Work out what it is and then fill in the missing numbers.

| 6 | 4 | 7 | 8 | 3 | 7 |
|---|---|---|---|---|---|
| 8 | 2 | 5 | 1 | 5 | 6 |
| 3 |   | 8 | 6 | 4 | 8 |
| 8 | 6 | 5 | 3 | 7 | 6 |
| 5 | 4 | 7 |   |   | 5 |
|   | 8 | 6 | 4 | 7 | 8 |

see answer
**66**

# Door Number Puzzle

Two workmen are putting the finishing touches to a new door they have fitted to house number 4761. All that is left to do is to screw the four metal digits to the door. Being a Mensan, Patrick could not resist challenging Bruce by asking him if he could screw the digits onto the door to give a four-figure number which could not be divided exactly by 9. When they had resolved that puzzle Bruce then asked Patrick if he could screw the same digits onto the door to give a four-figure number which could not be divided exactly by 3.

What are the answers to the two puzzles? Can either of them be done?

see answer
**81**

## Star Gazing

What is the largest star that can be drawn so that it is in the same proportions as the other stars and so that it does not touch another star or overlap the edges of the border?

see answer
**78**

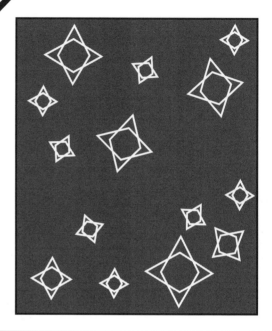

## Skyscraper Sizzler

A woman lives in a skyscraper 36 floors high and served by several elevators, which stop at each floor going up and down. Each morning she leaves her apartment on one of the floors and goes to one of the elevators. Whichever one she takes is three times more likely to be going up than down.

Why is this?

UP
DOWN

see answer
**69**

# Round the Hexagons

Can you work out what should be the contents of the top hexagon?

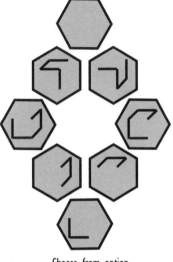

Choose from option

A B C D

see answer
68

# Water Divining

Two men are arguing about whether a square open-topped water tank is half full or not. How can they decide without removing the water or using any measuring device?

see answer
75

# Bartender's Beer

A man goes into a bar in New York. "Glass of beer" he says to the bartender. "Light or special?" asks the bartender. "What's the difference?" asks the man. "Light is 90 cents, special is $1," replies the bartender. "I'll have the special," says the man, placing $1 on the counter.

Another man comes into the bar. "Glass of beer please," he says, placing $1 on the counter. The bartender gives him the special.

Why does he do that?

see answer
**72**

# Pyramid Puzzle

Look at the sequence of shapes.
Which of the following options carries on the sequence?

A   B   C   D   E

see answer
**79**

# Ski-lift

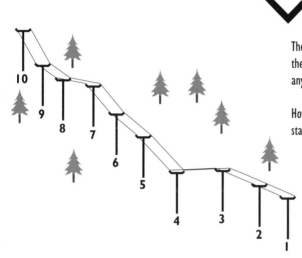

There are 10 places to embark and disembark on the ski-lift at the ski resort. It is possible to purchase a single ticket between any two stations.

How many different tickets are needed for skiers to go to every station from every other station?

*see answer*
**84**

# Round in Circles

Look at the four circles. Which of the following circles comes next in the sequence?

*see answer*
**110**

A    B    C    D    E

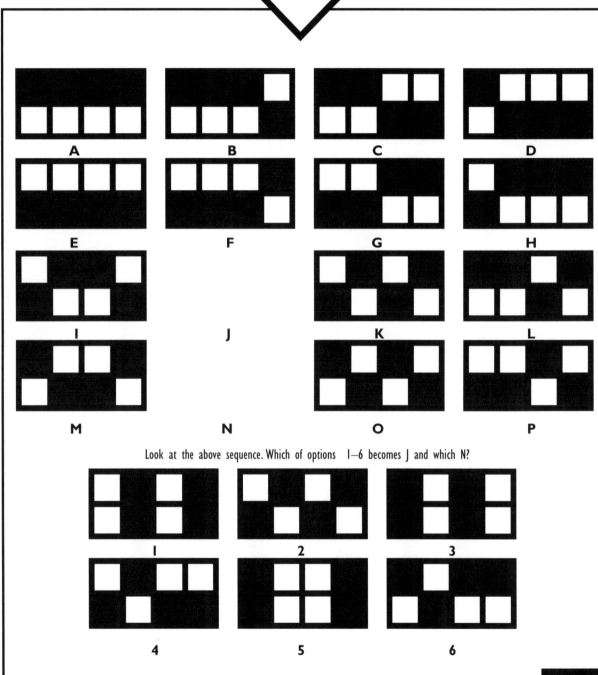

Look at the above sequence. Which of options 1–6 becomes J and which N?

see answer
**86**

Look at the pyramid. Which of the following symbols should replace the question mark?

A    B    C    D    E

*see answer*
**89**

# Pentagon Figures

What number should replace the question mark?

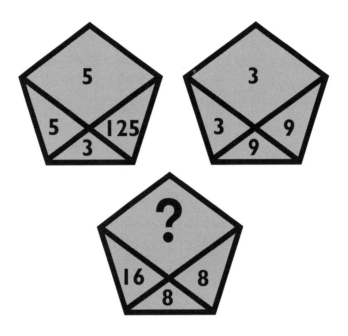

see answer
**101**

# Sun Shine

There is a valley somewhere on the Earth. The Sun is nearer the valley by over 4,800km at noon than it is when it rises or sets.

Where is this valley?

see answer
**91**

# Lonely Loser

Which of the following figures is the odd one out?

**A**

**B**

**C**

**D**

**E**

see answer
**96**

# Scratch Card

At the fairground there is a competition — you purchase a ticket on which there is a number of scratch-off squares. One square is marked "loser"; two others have identical symbols. If these appear before the loser square appears, you win a prize. The odds against winning are 2:1 against.

How many squares are there on the card?

see answer
**97**

# Work it Out

What number should replace the question mark?

see answer
94

# Dinner Party Placements

Mr and Mrs Ackrington, Mr and Mrs Blackpool, Mr and Mrs Chester and Mr and Mrs Doncaster are attending a dinner party. Only one couple does not sit next to each other, and this couple does not sit across from each other. The person sitting opposite Mrs Accrington is a man who is sitting immediately to the left of Mr Blackpool. The person sitting on Mrs Chester's immediate left is a man who is sitting across from Mr Doncaster.

Which couple does not sit next to each other?

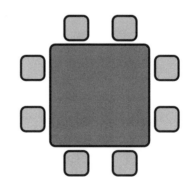

see answer
87

This grid consists of three squares marked A, B and C, and three squares marked 1, 2 and 3. The nine inner squares should incorporate the lines and symbols of both the letter and the number squares. One of the nine squares is incorrect. Which is it?

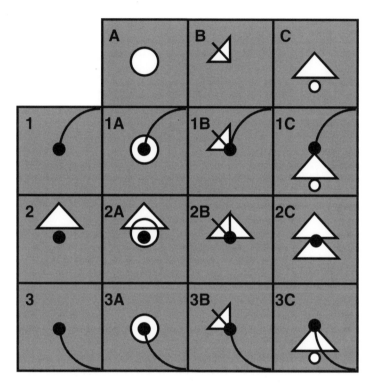

see answer
109

# Generation Gap

I am four times as old as my daughter. In 20 years time I shall be twice as old as her. How old are we today?

see answer
93

# Five Circles

All five circles have the same diameter. Draw a line moving through point A in such a way that it divides the five circles into two equal areas.

*see answer*
**105**

# Lateral Logic

Look at these shapes. Does option A, B, C, D or E continue the sequence?

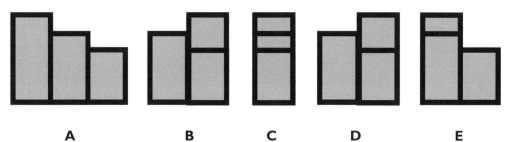

A     B     C     D     E

*see answer*
**99**

Look at the three squares. Does option A, B, C, D, E or F continue the sequence?

**A**     **B**     **C**     **D**

**E**     **F**

see answer
**92**

# Figure Columns

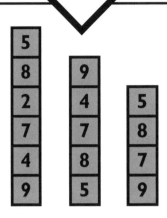

Look at the three columns of figures. Which column comes next in the sequence?

| 7 | | 8 | | 9 | | 9 |
|---|---|---|---|---|---|---|
| 8 | | 7 | | 8 | | 7 |
| 5 | | 9 | | 5 | | 8 |
| **A** | | **B** | | **C** | | **D** |

see answer
**90**

# Eighteen Trees

A gardener has 18 trees which he wishes to plant in straight rows of five trees per row. He sets himself the task of planting the 18 trees in such an arrangement that he will obtain the maximum number of rows of five trees per row.

There are two slightly different ways he can do this. Can you find both ways?

see answer
**103**

# Notable Number

Fill in the missing number. The last number is 7, not 8.

(99) (45) (39) (36) (28) (21)

(72) (27) (18) (21) (?) (13) (7)

see answer
**100**

# Counting Creatures

At the zoo there are penguins and huskies next to each other. In all, I can count 72 creatures and 200 legs.

How many penguins are there?

see answer
**102**

# Line Analogy

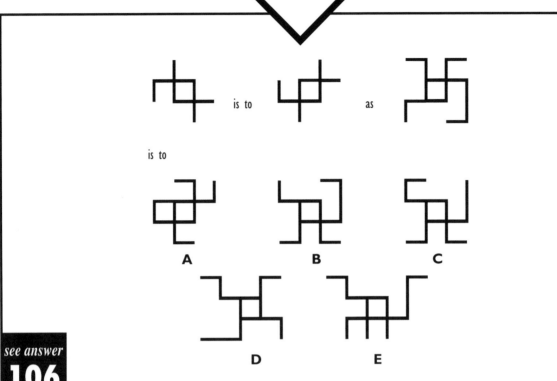

is to ... as ...

is to ...

A   B   C

D   E

see answer
**106**

# Chess Strategy

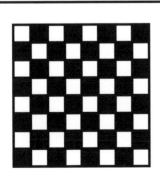

A man has to win two games of chess in a row in order to win a prize. In total, he has to play only three games, alternating between a strong and a weak opponent. Should he play strong, weak, strong; or weak, strong, weak?

see answer
**95**

# Careful Calculation

## 6128+9091

If the two numbers total 9825, what do the two numbers below total?

## 8159+1912

see answer
**88**

# Number Crunching

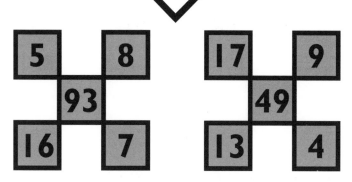

Look at the diagrams. What number should replace the question mark?

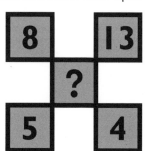

see answer
**108**

# Five Pilots

Five pilots take their flights from five different UK airports to five different countries.

Can you sort them out?

1. The aircraft from Stansted flies to Nice.
2. The flight from Cardiff has a captain named Paul.
3. Mike flies to JFK, New York, but not from Gatwick.
4. The flight from Manchester does not go to the USA.
5. Nick flies to Vancouver.
6. Paul does not fly to Roma.
7. Nick does not fly from Manchester.
8. Robin does not fly from Stansted.
9. The flight from Heathrow, not piloted by Tony, is not for Berlin.

| NAME | AIRPORT | DESTINATION |
|------|---------|-------------|
|      |         |             |
|      |         |             |
|      |         |             |
|      |         |             |
|      |         |             |

see answer
85

# Frogs and Flies

If 29 frogs catch 29 flies in 29 minutes, how many frogs are required to catch 87 flies in 87 minutes?

see answer
**98**

# Island Access

There is a lake with an island in the middle. On the island is a tree. The lake is deep and is 80 yards in diameter. There is another tree on the mainland. A non-swimmer wishes to get accross to the island, but all he has is a length of rope 300 yards long.

How does he get accross?

**TREE**

80 yards

● **TREE**

see answer
**107**

# Fairground Fiesta

At the carnival five boys of different ages eat different foods and take different rides.

1. Ron eats ice cream, Joe does not chew gum.
2. Sam, who is 14 years old, is not on the mountain.
3. The boy on the crocodile is 15 years old.
4. Len is not on the dodgems; Don is on the whirligig.
5. The boy eating ice cream is 13 years old.
6. The boy on the dodgems is eating a hot dog.
7. Joe eats fries on the big dipper.
8. Don, who is 12, is eating candy floss.

Work out the details of each boy.

|  |  | AGE | | | | | RIDE | | | | | FOOD | | | | |
|---|---|---|---|---|---|---|---|---|---|---|---|---|---|---|---|---|
|  |  | 11 | 12 | 13 | 14 | 15 | BIG DIPPER | DODGEMS | MOUNTAIN | WHIRLIGIG | CROCODILE | ICE CREAM | HOT DOG | CANDY FLOSS | FRIES | GUM |
| NAME | SAM |  |  |  |  |  |  |  |  |  |  |  |  |  |  |  |
|  | JOE |  |  |  |  |  |  |  |  |  |  |  |  |  |  |  |
|  | DON |  |  |  |  |  |  |  |  |  |  |  |  |  |  |  |
|  | LEN |  |  |  |  |  |  |  |  |  |  |  |  |  |  |  |
|  | RON |  |  |  |  |  |  |  |  |  |  |  |  |  |  |  |
| FOOD | ICE CREAM |  |  |  |  |  |  |  |  |  |  |  |  |  |  |  |
|  | HOT DOG |  |  |  |  |  |  |  |  |  |  |  |  |  |  |  |
|  | CANDY FLOSS |  |  |  |  |  |  |  |  |  |  |  |  |  |  |  |
|  | FRIES |  |  |  |  |  |  |  |  |  |  |  |  |  |  |  |
|  | GUM |  |  |  |  |  |  |  |  |  |  |  |  |  |  |  |
| RIDE | BIG DIPPER |  |  |  |  |  |  |  |  |  |  |  |  |  |  |  |
|  | DODGEMS |  |  |  |  |  |  |  |  |  |  |  |  |  |  |  |
|  | MOUNTAIN |  |  |  |  |  |  |  |  |  |  |  |  |  |  |  |
|  | WHIRLIGIG |  |  |  |  |  |  |  |  |  |  |  |  |  |  |  |
|  | CROCODILE |  |  |  |  |  |  |  |  |  |  |  |  |  |  |  |

| NAME | AGE | RIDE | FOOD |
|---|---|---|---|
|  |  |  |  |
|  |  |  |  |
|  |  |  |  |
|  |  |  |  |
|  |  |  |  |

see answer 104

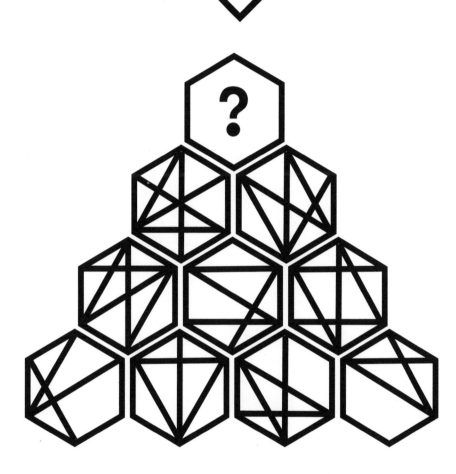

Look at the pyramid. From the following options, choose the contents of the top hexagon.

A        B        C        D        E

*see answer*
**116**

Look at the four circles. Should A, B, C, D or E follow on the sequence?

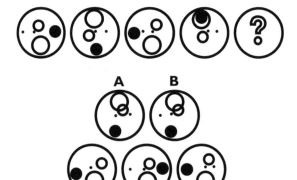

see answer
**111**

## Strange Series

see answer
**124**

Draw the next figure in this series.

# Suspicious Shape

Which of these shapes is the odd one out?

see answer
## 113

# Sequence Search

Look at the four circles. Which of the following options comes next in this sequence?

see answer
## 117

# Bird Fanciers

Five men from different countries each like a different bird. Each bird has a different collective noun.

1. Roger does not like plovers, which are not called a parliament.
2. The man who likes crows comes from France. This is not Edward, who is not from Scotland.
3. Albert likes owls; a group of starlings is called a murmuration.
4. Harold comes from Germany and likes ravens.
5. The man from England likes starlings.
6. Edward does not like the group called an unkindness of ravens.
7. The man who likes the group called murder comes from France.
8. Cameron is not from Belgium; Albert is not from Scotland.
9. The man who likes the group called wing is not from Germany.

Work out the details for each man.

| NAME | COUNTRY | BIRD | COLLECTIVE NOUN |
|------|---------|------|-----------------|
| | GERMANY / BELGIUM / FRANCE / ENGLAND / SCOTLAND | OWLS / PLOVERS / STARLINGS / CROWS / RAVENS | MURMURATION / WING / UNKINDNESS / MURDER / PARLIAMENT |

**NAME**
- ALBERT
- ROGER
- HAROLD
- CAMERON
- EDWARD

**COLLECTIVE NOUN**
- MURMURATION
- WING
- UNKINDNESS
- MURDER
- PARLIAMENT

**BIRD**
- OWLS
- PLOVERS
- STARLINGS
- CROWS
- RAVENS

| NAME | COUNTRY | BIRD | COLLECTIVE NOUN |
|------|---------|------|-----------------|
| | | | |
| | | | |
| | | | |
| | | | |
| | | | |

see answer 114

# Symbol Search

Each line and symbol which appears in the four outer circles is transferred to the middle circle according to a few rules. If a line or symbol occurs in the outer circles:
once, it is transferred;
twice, it is possibly transferred;
three times, it is transferred;
four times, it is not transferred.

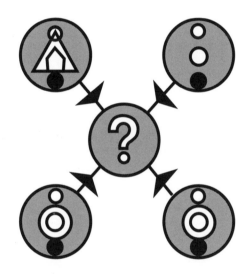

Which of the following circles should appear at the centre of the diagram?

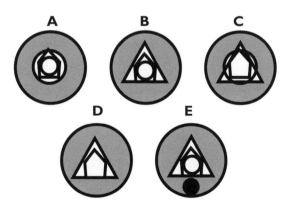

see answer
129

# Easy Equation

# 76=24

Correct this equation so that it makes sense by freely moving the given four digits but without introducing any additional mathematical symbols.

see answer
**112**

# Trying Trominoes

Consider the three trominoes. Now choose one of the following to accompany them.

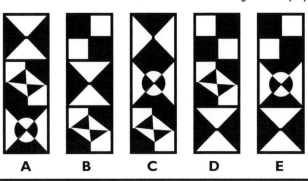

**A**　**B**　**C**　**D**　**E**

see answer
**119**

## Unwanted Guest

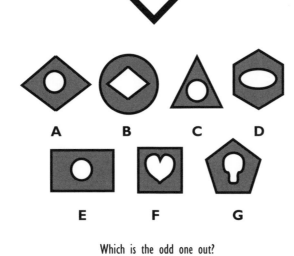

A     B     C     D

E     F     G

see answer
**127**

Which is the odd one out?

## Round the Circle

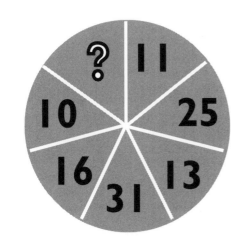

What is the missing number?

see answer
**121**

# Following Fun

Look at the sequence. Which of the following options comes next?

A

B

C

D

E

see answer
**128**

# Triangle Teaser

Work out the three missing numbers in the third triangle.

see answer
**122**

Five women each purchase a household item for use in a different room in their house.

1. Mrs Simpson does not keep her item in the bedroom.
2. Amy has a television; Mrs Griggs has a hi-fi.
3. Kylie does not keep her item in the bedroom.
4. Clara does not have a telephone.
5. Mrs Williams does not keep her item in the kitchen.
6. Kylie keeps hers in the conservatory.
7. Michelle has a bookcase; Mrs Dingle has a computer.
8. Michelle does not keep hers in the living room.
9. Mrs Pringle keeps hers in the study; Roxanne keeps hers in the kitchen.

Can you work out the full name of each woman, her item and where she keeps it?

| | FAMILYNAME | | | | | ITEM | | | | | ROOM | | | | |
|---|---|---|---|---|---|---|---|---|---|---|---|---|---|---|---|
| | WILLIAMS | SIMPSON | PRINGLE | DINGLE | GRIGGS | TELEVISION | BOOKCASE | HI-FI | COMPUTER | TELEPHONE | LIVING ROOM | KITCHEN | CONSERVATORY | BEDROOM | STUDY |
| **FIRST NAME** KYLIE | | | | | | | | | | | | | | | |
| AMY | | | | | | | | | | | | | | | |
| CLARA | | | | | | | | | | | | | | | |
| MICHELLE | | | | | | | | | | | | | | | |
| ROXANNE | | | | | | | | | | | | | | | |
| **ROOM** LIVING ROOM | | | | | | | | | | | | | | | |
| KITCHEN | | | | | | | | | | | | | | | |
| CONSERVATORY | | | | | | | | | | | | | | | |
| BEDROOM | | | | | | | | | | | | | | | |
| STUDY | | | | | | | | | | | | | | | |
| **ITEM** TELEVISION | | | | | | | | | | | | | | | |
| BOOKCASE | | | | | | | | | | | | | | | |
| HI-FI | | | | | | | | | | | | | | | |
| COMPUTER | | | | | | | | | | | | | | | |
| TELEPHONE | | | | | | | | | | | | | | | |

| | | | |
|---|---|---|---|
| | | | |
| | | | |
| | | | |
| | | | |
| | | | |

**see answer 118**

# Sticky Business

A stick breaks into three pieces. Without measuring the pieces or actually attempting to construct a triangle, how can you quickly determine whether they will form a triangle?

see answer
**125**

# Little and Large

Which is the odd one out?
A B C D E

see answer
**130**

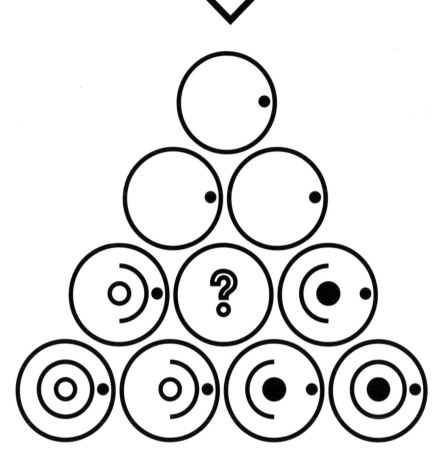

Consider the pyramid. Which of the following five options replaces the question mark?

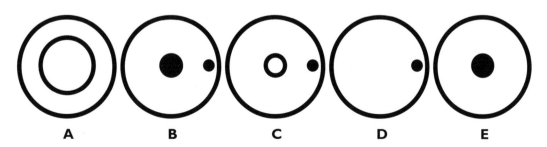

A    B    C    D    E

*see answer*
**120**

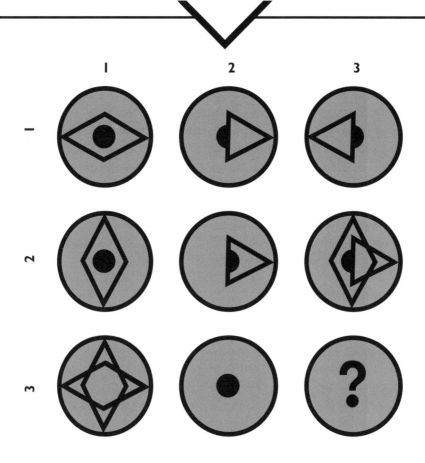

Which circle fits into the blank space to carry on the pattern?

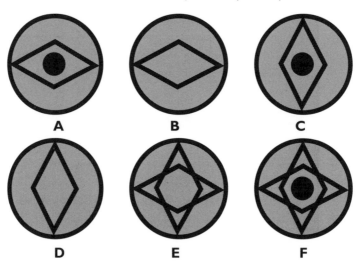

see answer
**115**

# Gritty Grid

Each of the nine squares in the grid marked 1A to 3C should incorporate all the lines and symbols shown in the squares of the same letter and number. For example, 3C should incorporate the shapes in 3 and C.

One of the squares is incorrect. Which is it?

see answer
123

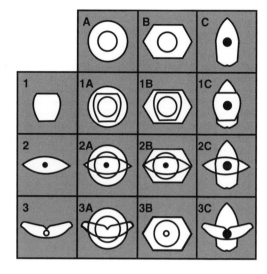

# Fancy Figures

Find a logical reason for arranging these numbers into four groups of three numbers each:
**106  168  181  217  218  251  349  375  433  457  532  713**

| GROUP 1 | GROUP 2 | GROUP 3 | GROUP 4 |
|---------|---------|---------|---------|
|         |         |         |         |
|         |         |         |         |
|         |         |         |         |

see answer
126

## Answer 1
### Las Vegas
Each gambler's die was numbered as follows:
Diablo:  6 – 1 – 8 – 6 – 1 – 8
Scarface:  7 – 5 – 3 – 7 – 5 – 3
Lucky:  2 – 9 – 4 – 2 – 9 – 4
In a long run:
Diablo would win against Scarface 10 times in 18;
Scarface would win against Lucky 10 times in 18;
Lucky would win against Diablo 10 times in 18.

Diablo v Scarface: 6–7; 1–7; 8–7 win; 6–5 win; 1–5;
8–5 win; 6–3 win; 1–3; 8–3 win, which, when
repeated, gives 10 wins and 8 losses for Diablo.
Scarface v Lucky: 7–2 win; 5–2 win; 3–2 win; 7–9; 5–9;
3–9; 7–4 win; 5–4 win; 3–4, which, when repeated,
gives 10 wins and 8 losses for Scarface.
Lucky v Diablo:  2–6; 9 – 6 win; 4–6; 2–1 win; 9–1 win;
4–1 win; 2–8; 9–8 win; 4–8, which, when repeated,
gives 10 wins and 8 losses to Lucky.

## Answer 2
### Three Circles

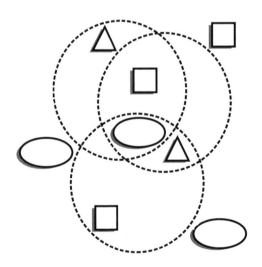

## Answer 3
### Town Clock
I forgot to mention that my clock was digital. One
line was not functioning on the eight lines that make
up each digit.

◀ THIS LINE
NOT FUNCTIONING

| | TIME SHOWED | SHOULD HAVE SHOWN |
|---|---|---|
| 8.55 | 5 | 5 |
| 8.56 | 6 | 6 |
| 8.58 | 6 ◀ MISSING | 8 |
| 8.59 | 5 ◀ MISSING | 9 |
| 9.00 | 0 ◀ MISSING | 0 |

## Answer 4
### Booth Bonanza
If number eight did not require repairing the
supervisor would have said that five out of the first
seven needed repairing.

## Answer 5
### Tricky Triangles
E. There are four triangles constantly moving
clockwise around the arms and visiting points in
sequence.

### Answer 6
### Murder in Mind
Alf Muggins. If it was Jack Vicious, the statements of Alf Muggins and Jim Pouncer would be true. If it was Sid Shifty, the statements of Jack Vicious, Alf Muggins and Jim Pouncer would be true. If it was Jim Pouncer, the statements of Sid Shifty and Alf Muggins would be true. Therefore it is Alf Muggins, and only the statement of Jim Pouncer is true.

### Answer 7
### Fancy Figures
2, 5, 7, 10, 12, 15, 17.

### Answer 8
### Hexagon Harmony
A. There are six triangles, each with their base on one of the sides of the hexagon. Each triangle increases in height by a quarter of the width of the hexagon at each stage. So, showing one triangle only:

### Answer 9
### Manor House

| Name | Occupation | Pastime | Rest day |
|------|-----------|---------|----------|
| Smith | Butler | Squash | Friday |
| Jones | Gardener | Golf | Tuesday |
| Wood | Chauffeur | Fishing | Wednesday |
| Clark | Janitor | Chess | Thursday |
| James | Cook | Bridge | Monday |

### Answer 10
### Converging Circles
C.

### Answer 11
### Sears Tower
450m.

### Answer 12
### Land of Zoz

| What they say they are | Numbers in the group | What they actually are | What they become |
|------------------------|----------------------|------------------------|------------------|
| Fibkins | 30 | 30 Switchkins | 30 Fibkins |
| Switchkins | 15:15 | 15 Fibkins<br>15 Switchkins | 15 Fibkins |
| Truthkins | 10:10:10 | 10 Truthkins<br>10 Fibkins<br>10 Switchkins | 10 Fibkins |

Therefore 55 Fibkins live in pentagonal houses that night.

If Truthkins only tell the truth, then it must be that they are in the group of 3 x 10. This group made the statement "We are all Truthkins." The Switchkins must be the group of 30 x 1, which lied "We are all Fibkins", thus becoming Fibkins – it could not be Fibkins making this statement because they always lie while Truthkins only tell the truth. This means that the other statement was made by 15 x 2 of Switchkins and Fibkins. Therefore, there are 55 Fibkins (10 who lie about being Truthkins, the 15 who claimed to be Switchkins and the 30 former Switchkins who became Fibkins by claiming they were Fibkins).

### Answer 13
### Making Eyes
D.
There is a sequence occurring from the right eye to the left eye (as we look at them). Look at stages one and two. The contents of the eyes in stage one have merged to form the left eye of stage two and a new symbol has been introduced in the right eye of stage two. Now look at stages two and three. The contents of the left eye in stage two has moved away and does not appear in stage three. The symbol from the right eye in stage two has moved to fill the left eye of stage three and a new symbol has been introduced in the right eye of stage three. This pattern of change is then continued, so that the left eye of stage four contains a merging of both eyes in stage three.

## Answer 14
### Shooting Range
Colonel Present scored 200 ( 60, 60, 40, 40)
Major Aim scored 240 (60, 60, 60, 60)
General Fire scored 180 (60, 40, 40, 40)

The incorrect statements made by each marksman are as follows:
Colonel Present, statement no. 1;
Major Aim, statement no. 3;
General Fire, statement no. 3.

## Answer 15
### Counterfeit Coins
Only one weighing operation is necessary. You take one coin from bag one, two coins from bag two and three coins from bag three and weigh all six coins together. If they weigh 305g the first bag contains the counterfeit coins; if they weigh 310g the second bag does, and if they weigh 315g the third bag does.

## Answer 16
### Sitting Pretty

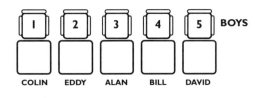

COLIN  EDDY  ALAN  BILL  DAVID

HILARY  FIONA  INDIRA  JANE  GRACE

## Answer 17
### Figure of Fun
C.
The number of right angles in each figure increases by one each time.

## Answer 18
### House Hunting
We have to find a unique number which will answer three of the questions.

1. Is it under 41?

No 41–82

Yes 1-40

2. Is it divisible by 4?

| Yes | 44 | 48 | 52 | 56 | 60 | 64 | 68 | 72 | 76 | 80 |
|---|---|---|---|---|---|---|---|---|---|---|
| No | 41 | 42 | 43 | 45 | 46 | 47 | 49 | 50 | 51 | 53 |
|  | 54 | 55 | 57 | 58 | 59 | 61 | 62 | 63 | 65 | 66 |
|  | 67 | 69 | 70 | 71 | 73 | 74 | 75 | 77 | 78 | 79 |
|  | 81 | 82 |  |  |  |  |  |  |  |  |
| Yes | 4 | 8 | 12 | 16 | 20 | 24 | 28 | 32 | 36 | 40 |
| No | 1 | 2 | 3 | 5 | 6 | 7 | 9 | 10 | 11 | 13 |
|  | 14 | 15 | 17 | 18 | 19 | 21 | 22 | 23 | 25 | 26 |
|  | 27 | 29 | 30 | 31 | 33 | 34 | 35 | 37 | 38 | 39 |

3. Is is a square number?

Yes  64 unique

| No | 44 | 48 | 52 | 56 | 60 | 68 | 72 | 76 | 80 |  |  |
|---|---|---|---|---|---|---|---|---|---|---|---|
| Yes | 49 | 81 |  |  |  |  |  |  |  |  |  |
| No | 41 | 42 | 43 | 45 | 46 | 47 | 50 | 51 | 53 |  |  |
|  | 54 | 55 | 57 | 58 | 59 | 61 | 62 | 63 | 65 | 66 |  |
|  | 67 | 69 | 70 | 71 | 73 | 74 | 75 | 77 | 78 | 79 | 82 |
| Yes | 4 | 16 | 36 |  |  |  |  |  |  |  |  |
| No | 8 | 12 | 20 | 24 | 28 | 32 | 40 |  |  |  |  |
| Yes | 1 | 9 | 25 |  |  |  |  |  |  |  |  |
| No | 2 | 3 | 5 | 6 | 7 | 10 | 11 | 13 |  |  |  |
|  | 14 | 15 | 17 | 18 | 19 | 21 | 22 | 23 |  |  |  |
|  | 26 | 27 | 29 | 30 | 31 | 33 | 34 | 35 | 37 | 38 | 39 |

By answering no to the first question, yes to the second and yes to the third you arrive at a unique number – 64, which is therefore the number of Archibald's house.

### Answer 19
### Dynamic Dog

22½ miles. Work out how long it takes Russell Carter to walk home. Spot has been running all this time at his given constant speed so it is simple to work out how many miles Spot has covered during this period.

Russell walks for 10 miles at 4mph, taking 2½ hours. Spot is running for 2½ hours too, at 9mph, which means he covers 22½ miles.

### Answer 20
### Roving Robot

There was a stationary car parked 5 m to the robot's right. The program should have said "moving land vehicle".

### Answer 21
### Dazzling Diamond

### Answer 22
### Japan Hotel

"Push" on one side; "Pull" on the other side.

### Answer 23
### Salary Increase

At first glance the best option seems to be the first. However, the second option works out best.

| First option | ($500 increase after each 12 months) |
|---|---|
| First year | $10,000 + $10,000 = $20,000 |
| Second year | $10,250 + $10,250 = $20,500 |
| Third year | $10,500 + $10,500 = $21,000 |
| Fourth year | $10,750 + $10,750 = $21,500 |

| Second option | ($125 increase after each 6 months) |
|---|---|
| First year | $10,000 + $10,125 = $20,125 |
| Second year | $10,250 + $10,375 = $20,625 |
| Third year | $10,500 + $10,625 = $21,125 |
| Fourth year | $10,750 + $10,875 = $21,625 |

### Answer 24
### Funny Fingers

Let us assume that 240 fingers could be 20 aliens with 12 fingers each or 12 aliens with 20 fingers each, etc. This does not provide a unique answer so eliminates all numbers that can be factorized.

Now consider prime numbers: there could be one alien with 229 fingers (not allowed, according to sentence one); 229 aliens with one finger (not according to sentence two). Again, this does not provide a unique answer so eliminates all prime numbers except those squared. There is only one of these between 200 and 300 and that is 289 ($17^2$). So in the room are 17 aliens each with 17 fingers.

### Answer 25
**Pick a Pattern**
C. The middle pattern is removed and encases the outer pattern of the original figure.

### Answer 26
**Barrels of Fun**
The 40-gallon barrel contains beer. The first customer purchases the 30-gallon and 36-gallon barrels, giving 66 gallon of wine. The second customer purchases 132 gallons of wine – the 32-gallon, 38-gallon and 62-gallon barrels. The 40-gallon barrel has not been purchased by either customer and therefore contains the beer.

### Answer 27
**Mouse Moves**
As there are 216 chambers – an even number – there is no central chamber. The task is therefore impossible.

### Answer 28
**Treasured Trees**

| Tree | Elm | Ash | Beech | Lime | Poplar |
|---|---|---|---|---|---|
| Person | Bill | Jim | Tony | Sylvester | Desmond |
| Club | Squash | Golf | Tennis | Bowling | Soccer |
| Bird | Owl | Blackbird | Crow | Robin | Starling |
| Year | 1970 | 1971 | 1972 | 1973 | 1974 |

### Answer 29
**Intergalactic Ingenuity**
The wife of M9 is F10. The male speaker on nuclear fission is M3.

| Male | M1 | M3 | M5 | M9 | M7 |
|---|---|---|---|---|---|
| Female | F8 | F6 | F4 | F10 | F2 |
| Vehicle | Warp distorter | Galaxy freighter | Space oscillator | Nebula accelerator | Astro carrier |
| Speech | Time travel | Nuclear fission | Astral transporting | Mind reading | Anti-gravity |
| Feature | 12 fingers | 3 eyes | 3 legs | 4 arms | Webbed feet |

### Answer 30
**Handkerchief Challenge**
Charlie puts the handkerchief under a door and stands on the corner at the other side.

### Answer 31
**Algarve Rendezvous**

On the corner of road 5, street 4. Draw a line down the person who is in the middle on the roads axis. Then draw a line across the person who is in the middle of the streets axis.

### Answer 32
**Searching Segments**

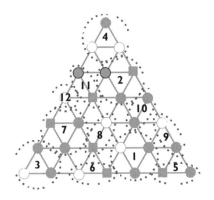

## Answer 33
### Take a Tile
**B.**

Looking both across and down, any lines common to the first two tiles disappear in the third tile.

## Answer 34
### Prisoners' Porridge

2519 prisoners.

2519 divided by 3 = 839 tables with 2 over
2519 divided by 5 = 503 tables with 4 over
2519 divided by 7 = 359 with 6 over
2519 divided by 9 = 279 with 8 over
2519 divided by 11 = 229 exactly.

## Answer 35
### Creative Circles
**A.** Looking both across and down, the contents of the third square are formed by merging the contents of the two previous squares as follows:

one white or black circle remains;
two black circles become white;
two white circles become black.

## Answer 36
### Think of a Number
Anastasia tells a lie when she says that the number is below 500. The only square and cube between 99 and 999 whose first and last digit is 5, 7 or 9 is 729.

## Answer 37
### Dog Delight
The dalmations are called Andy (owned by Bill) and Donald (owned by Colin).

## Answer 38
### Club Conundrum
2. If all 49 women wore glasses then 21 men wore glasses too. If 11 of these men were under 20 years of age, only 10 men older than 20 years of age wore glasses. Then 10 – 8 = 2 men is the minimum number.

## Answer 39
### Three Squares

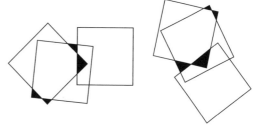

**D.**
The three squares form four triangles.

## Answer 40
### Roulette Riddle
15.

## Answer 41
### Tree Teaser
Spencer prunes six more trees than Don.

## Answer 42
### Girl Talk

| The three ages, when multiplied, must be one of the following combinations: | When added, they equal |
|---|---|
| 72 x 1 x 1 | 74 |
| 36 x 2 x 1 | 39 |
| 18 x 4 x 1 | 23 |
| 9 x 4 x 2 | 15 |
| 9 x 8 x 1 | 18 |
| 6 x 6 x 2 | 14 |
| 8 x 3 x 3 | 14 |
| 12 x 6 x 1 | 19 |
| 12 x 3 x 2 | 17 |
| 18 x 2 x 2 | 22 |
| 6 x 3 x 4 | 13 |
| 3 x 24 x 1 | 28 |

The census-taker should have known the number of the house, as he could see it, but he did not know their ages, therefore the house must be number 14. He needed more information to decide whether their ages were 6, 6, 2 or 8, 3, 3. When the woman says "eldest" daughter, he knows they were 8, 3, 3.

### Answer 43
### Lucid Lines
E.
The two figures merge into one by superimposing one onto the other, except that when two lines appear in the same position they disappear.

### Answer 44
### Number Placement

| | | | |
|---|---|---|---|
| ② | 14 | 10 | 7 |
| 9 | 6 | ① | 4 |
| 16 | ③ | 13 | 11 |
| 12 | 8 | 5 | 15 |

So that:
1. **No two consecutive numbers appear in any horizontal, vertical or diagonal line;**
2. **No two consecutive numbers appear in adjacent squares.**

### Answer 45
### Play Watching

 MR

ⓒ MRS

### Answer 46
### Suspicious Circles
E. A is a mirror image of C; B is a mirror image of D.

### Answer 47
### Study Time
Anne studies algebra, history, French and Japanese.
Bess studies physics, English, French and Japanese.
Candice studies algebra, physics, English and history.

### Answer 48
### Tricky Triangles

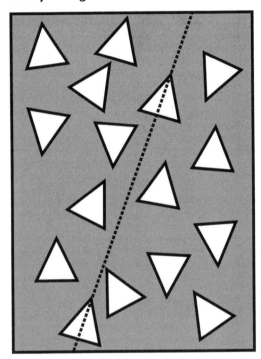

Two segments: all the triangles do not need to be the same size.

### Answer 49
### Picking Professions
Mr Carter is the drover.

## Answer 50
### Great Golfers

Edward Peters; Robert Edwards; Peter Roberts. Mr Peters must be Edward because the man who spoke last is Robert and he is not Mr Peters.

## Answer 51
### Lost Time

11 + 12 + 1 + 2 = 26
10 + 3 + 9 + 4 = 26
5 + 6 + 7 + 8 = 26.

## Answer 52
### Pleased Pupils

| Name | Class | Subject | Sport |
|------|-------|---------|-------|
| Alice | 6 | Algebra | Squash |
| Betty | 2 | Biology | Running |
| Clara | 4 | History | Swimming |
| Doris | 3 | Geography | Tennis |
| Elizabeth | 5 | Chemistry | Basketball |

## Answer 53
### Hello Sailor

| Name | Rank | Ship | Location |
|------|------|------|----------|
| Perkins | Steward | Aircraft carrier | Malta |
| Ward | Seaman | Cruiser | Portsmouth |
| Manning | Commander | Submarine | Falklands |
| Dewhurst | Purser | Frigate | Gibraltar |
| Brand | Captain | Warship | Crete |

## Answer 54
### Gone Fishing

North ◄──────── Pier ────────► South

| Name | Joe | Fred | Dick | Henry | Malcolm |
|------|-----|------|------|-------|---------|
| Occupation | Banker | Electrician | Professor | Plumber | Salesman |
| Town | L.A. | Orlando | Tucson | New York | St Louis |
| Bait | Worms | Bread | Maggots | Shrimps | Meal |
| Catch | 6 | 15 | 10 | 9 | 1 |

## Answer 55
### Winning Wager

It is possible but there has to be a compensating factor. Jim has $8 at the start so Bill can win only $8 even if he wins all 10 frames. Jim, however, can win a large sum if he wins every frame: $8, $12, $18, $27, etc. Therefore, to compensate, Bill can win a small amount even if he wins fewer frames than Jim. If makes no difference in the winning order of frames.

| Frame | Jim | Jim has $8 |
|-------|-----|-----------|
| 1 | win | $12.00 |
| 2 | lose | $6.00 |
| 3 | lose | $3.00 |
| 4 | win | $4.50 |
| 5 | win | $6.75 |
| 6 | lose | $3.38 |
| 7 | win | $5.07 |
| 8 | win | $7.60 |
| 9 | win | $11.40 |
| 10 | lose | $5.70 = loses $2.30 from starting $8.00 |

## Answer 56
### Odd One Out

E. In all the others, if the line dividing the square is a mirror the correct mirror image has been shown.

### Answer 57
### Spot the Shape
1A.

### Answer 58
### Table Talk

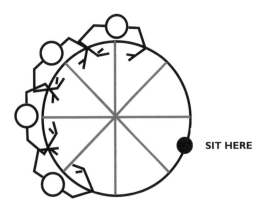

SIT HERE

Mark four points exactly opposite each of the four people. Now count the number of points that lie between each pair. The place to sit is midway between the points. This principle works for any seating plan.

### Answer 59
### Changing Trains
25 minutes. As the man leaves home according to his normal schedule it is earlier than 6.30 pm when he picks up his wife. As the total journey saves 10 minutes, that must be the same time it takes the man from the point he picks up his wife to the station and back to the same point. Assuming that it takes an equal five minutes each way he has therefore picked up his wife five minutes before he would normally, which means 6.20pm. So his wife must have walked from 6.00pm to 6.25pm, that is for 25 minutes.

### Answer 60
### Fathers and Daughters

| Father | Daughter | Father's age | Daughter's age |
|--------|----------|--------------|----------------|
| John | Alison | 52 | 20 |
| Kevin | Diana | 53 | 19 |
| Len | Betty | 50 | 21 |
| Malcolm | Eve | 54 | 18 |
| Nick | Carol | 51 | 17 |

### Answer 61
### Sums about Sons
Graham is 9 years old and Frederick is 27. Thus, 27 squared is the same as 9 cubed = 729. There are 18 steps, 36 palisades and 243 bricks, which, when added together, gives the door number of 297.

### Answer 62
### Cube Diagonals

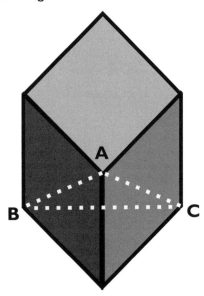

60°. If a third face diagonal, BC, is drawn this completes an equilateral triangle. All its sides are equal because they are cube diagonals. Being equilateral, all its angles are 60°.

## Answer 63
### Best Beer

18 days. If it takes a man 27 days to drink one barrel, he drinks 0.037 of a barrel each day. Similarly, a woman drinks 0.0185 of a barrel each day. Added together, a day's combined drinking consumes 0.0555 of a barrel. In this case, to drink the whole barrel takes 18.018 days.

## Answer 64
### Circles and Triangles

C. Each horizontal line and vertical column contains the wavy shape shown once vertical and once black. Similarly, each line and column shows the triangle three times: once pointing left, once right, once down.

## Answer 65
### Gun Running

The total number of dollars that they receive for their cattle must be a square number. They buy an odd number of sheep at $10 each, so the tens figure in the total square number must be an odd number. The only square numbers with an odd "tens" figure have "6" as their "units" figure.

The number 256 is one such number, equalling the price of 16 steer at $16 a head as well 25 sheep at $10 a head with $6 for the goat. Bully Bill evens up the takings by giving Dynamo Dan a goat (worth $6) and the Colt .45 to equal his own share of the sheep ($10) minus the Colt .45. Therefore the gun is worth $2.

## Answer 66
### Missing Numbers

The grid should contain 1x1, 2x2, 3x3, 4x4, 5x5, 6x6, 7x7, 8x8. Therefore, the missing numbers are 2, 7, 8, 8. All the numbers are placed so that two identical numbers are never adjacent.

## Answer 67
### Rifle Range

Major Mustard. Tabulate the results so that each set equals 71. There are only three possible ways to do this: 25, 20, 20, 3,2,1; 25, 20, 10, 10, 5, 1; and 50, 10, 5, 3, 2, 1. The first set is Colonel Ketchup's (since 22 cannot be scored in two shots in the other sets); the third set is Major Mustard's (as we know that he scores 3). So Major Mustard hit the bull's eye.

## Answer 68
### Round the Hexagons

C.

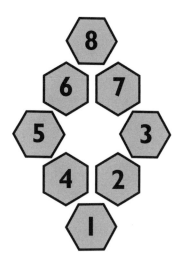

The third hexagon is formed by merging hexagons 1 and 2. The fifth hexagon is formed by merging hexagons 4 and 1. In this way, the hexagons build up the shape along vertical lines going from the bottom hexagon upwards. Continuing this trend, the top hexagon is formed by a merging of hexagons 3, 5, 6, and 7: the two straight lines moving upwards to the top hexagon.

### Answer 69
### Skyscraper Sizzler
She lives on the 27th floor. The elevator came down from the 36th to the 28th floor – 9 floors; or it came up from the first to the 27th floor – 27 floors. Therefore there is a 3:1 chance of it going up than down.

### Answer 70
### Black and White Balls
Three chances in four. Look at the possible combinations of drawing the balls. There are black–black; white–black; black–white; and white–white. The only one of the four possible combinations in which it does not occur is the fourth one. The chances of drawing at least one black ball are, therefore, three in four.

### Answer 71
### Carrier Pigeons
No. The pigeons remain at 200lbs even whilst flying. Those flying up would reduce the weight, but those flying down would increase the weight, so balancing the total weight.

### Answer 72
### Bartender's Beer
The first man places a $1 bill on the counter. The second man puts down three quarters, two dimes and a nickel – amounting to one dollar. Had he wanted a 90-cent beer he had the change to offer the exact amount.

### Answer 73
### Logical Clocks
A. At each stage the big hand moves anti-clockwise first by 10 minutes, then 20 and, finally, by 30 minutes (option A). At each stage the small hand moves clockwise first by one hour, then two hours and, finally, three hours (option A).

### Answer 74
### Broadway, NY
The fact that the man does not see a door (as in the illustration) indicates that the door must be on the other side – the kerb side. As this is New York, the bus is therefore moving to A.

### Answer 75
### Water Divining

By lifting the water tank onto its near-side edge.
If you cannot see the far edge then the tank is more than half full.
If you can just see the far edge then the tank is exactly half full.
If you can see below the far edge then the tank is less than half full.

## Answer 76
### Missing Links

1. In the first bar, 7 x 4 x 8 x 8 x 2 = 3584.
Similarly, 3 x 5 x 8 x 4 = 480.
Following the same formula, the missing number in the second bar is 2268 and, in the third, 2688 and 768.

2. In the first bar 58 x 2 = 116.
In the same vein, 16 x 1 = 16. Using the same formula, the missing number in the second bar is 657 and, in the third, 162 and 72.

## Answer 77
### City Slicker

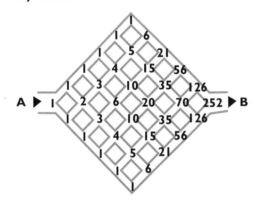

252. Each number represents the number of possible routes to each intersection.

## Answer 78
### Star Gazing

## Answer 79
### Pyramid Puzzle
**D.**
Each pair of circles produces the circle above by carrying forward only those elements that are different. Similar elements disappear.

## Answer 80
## Round and Round the Garden

10m

10m

(Not to scale)

49m.
A = 9m  B = 8m  C = 8m  D = 6m  E = 6m  F = 4m
G = 4m  H = 2m  I = 2m = TOTAL 49m

## Answer 81
## Door Number Puzzle
No in both cases, except if the 6 is turned upside down into a 9. If the numbers were 1, 4, 7 and 9, it could never be divisible by 9 but always by 3.

## Answer 82
## Dice Dilemma
No. 3.

## Answer 83
## Triangles and Trapeziums
A.
The figures change places so that the one in front goes to the back and vice versa.

## Answer 84
## Ski-lift
90.
You can buy nine tickets from each of the 10 stations: 9 x 10 = 90.

## Answer 85
## Five Pilots

| Name | Airport | Destination |
| --- | --- | --- |
| Mike | Heathrow | JFK |
| Nick | Gatwick | Vancouver |
| Paul | Cardiff | Berlin |
| Robin | Manchester | Roma |
| Tony | Stansted | Nice |

## Answer 86
## Making Moves
J is option 4; N is option 6. The black segments move from top to bottom and right to left in sequence, then rise in the same way. However, when an arrangement has occurred previously it is omitted from the sequence.

## Answer 87
## Dinner Party Placements
Mr and Mrs Chester.

## Answer 88
## Careful Calculation
8679.
Turn the page upside-down and add up the two numbers.

## Answer 89
## Pyramidal Logic.
E. Each symbol is linked to the two below it. No symbol never appears above an identical one. The symbols are produced as follows:

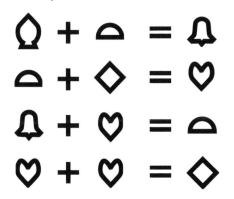

so that ▦ + ♀ must equal something completely different to anything above. Of the options shown, this can only be ♧.

## Answer 90
## Figure Columns
D. The smallest number is dropped each time and the remaining numbers appear in reverse order.

## Answer 91
## Sun Shine

Any valley on or near the equator, owing to the revolution of the Earth.

## Answer 92
## Shady Squares
C.
The square turns 90° clockwise at each stage. Similarly, the shading also moves one segment clockwise at each stage.

## Answer 93
## Generation Gap
I am 40 and my daughter is 10.

## Answer 94
## Work it Out
24. In the first circle, 56 + 79 divided by 5 = 27. The same formula applies to circles two and three.

## Answer 95
## Chess Strategy
Strong, weak, strong. He will always beat the weak player, so playing this way gives him two chances to beat the strong one.

## Answer 96
## Lonely Loser
E.
The others all have rotated symmetry. In other words, if they were rotated through 180° they would appear exactly the same.

## Answer 97
## Scratch Card
The number of squares on the card is immaterial. The odds are always 2:1 against.

## Answer 98
## Frogs and Flies
29.

## Answer 99
### Lateral Logic
B.
There are three sizes of rectangle. In the next three stages **A** moves from left to right one stage at a time. Then it is the turn of **B** to do the same.

## Answer 100
### Missing Number
12.
The third number, 27, is obtained by adding the digits of the two preceding numbers – 7 + 2 + 9 + 9. This formula applies throughout the puzzle.

## Answer 101
### Pentagon Figures
4. In the first pentagon 5 x 5 x 125 = 3125 or $5^5$. In the second pentagon, 3 x 9 x 9 = 243 or $3^5$. In the same way, 16 x 8 x 8 = 1024 or $4^5$.

## Answer 102
### Counting Creatures
44.
28 huskies with four legs each plus 44 penguins with two each, making 200 in all.

## Answer 103
### Eighteen Trees

Solution 1

Solution 2

Both solutions produce nine rows of five trees per row.

## Answer 104
### Fairground Fiesta

| Name | Age | Ride | Food |
|------|-----|------|------|
| Sam | 14 | Dodgems | Hot dog |
| Joe | 11 | Big dipper | Fries |
| Don | 12 | Whirligig | Candy floss |
| Len | 15 | Crocodile | Gum |
| Ron | 13 | Mountain | Ice cream |

## Answer 105
## Five Circles

## Answer 106
## Line Analogy
B. The figures are flipped vertically.

## Answer 107
## Island Access

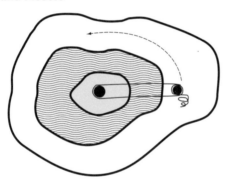

He ties the rope to the tree, then walks around the lake carrying the rope. As he reaches half-way, the rope wraps itself around the tree on the island. He then ties the rope to the tree on the mainland and hauls himself across to the island.

## Answer 108
## Number Crunching
33.
Multiply diagonally opposite squares and subtract the smaller product from the larger:
(13 x 5) - (8 x 4) = 33.

## Answer 109
## Square Sort
2C.

## Answer 110
## Round in Circles
C.
The striped and black segments are moving in the following sequences: the striped segments move two anti-clockwise then one clockwise in turn, and continue in this way. The black segments move two clockwise then one anti-clockwise in turn, and continue in this way too.

## Answer 111
## Logic Circles
D.
The large circle moves 180°; the small white circle moves 180°; the black circle moves 90°; and the black dot moves 180°.

## Answer 112
## Easy Equation
$7^2 = 49$. The 6 has been turned over to convert it into a 9 and the 2 becomes a square.

## Answer 113
## Suspicious Shape
B.
A and F are the same, as are C and D, and E and G.

## Answer 114
## Bird Fanciers

| Name | Country | Birds | Collective Noun |
|------|---------|-------|-----------------|
| Albert | Belgium | Owls | Parliament |
| Roger | France | Crows | Murder |
| Harold | Germany | Ravens | Unkindness |
| Cameron | Scotland | Plovers | Wing |
| Edward | England | Starlings | Murmuration |

## Answer 115
### Perpetuate the Pattern
**F.**
Column 1 is added to column 2 to make column 3.
Similarly, line 1 is added to line 2 to make line 3. In
both cases, repeated symbols disappear.

## Answer 116
### Hexagonal Pyramid
**E.**
The contents of each hexagon are determined by
merging the contents of the two hexagons
immediately below, except that two identical lines
disappear.

## Answer 117
### Sequence Search
**D.**

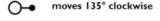

moves 135° clockwise

moves 45° clockwise

moves 90° clockwise

moves 180°

## Answer 118
### Household Items

| First name | Family name | Room | Appliance |
|---|---|---|---|
| Kylie | Dingle | Conservatory | Computer |
| Amy | Williams | Bedroom | Television |
| Clara | Griggs | Living Room | Hi-fi |
| Roxanne | Simpson | Kitchen | Telephone |
| Michelle | Pringle | Study | Bookcase |

## Answer 119
### Trying Trominoes
**B.**
There are four different symbols grouped ABC,
ABD, BCD and, in option B, ACD.

A      B      C      D

**Answer 120**
**Pyramid Plot**
D.
Each pair of circles produces the circle above by carrying on elements that they have in common. Different elements disappear.

**Answer 121**
**Round the Circle**
20.
Start at 10 and jump to alternate segments, adding 1, then 2, then 3 and so on.

**Answer 122**
**Triangle Teaser**

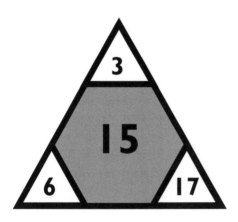

Divide the central number by 5 to give the top number. Add the digits of the central number to give the bottom left number. Reverse the digits of the central number and divide by three to give the bottom right number.

**Answer 123**
**Gritty Grid**
3A.

**Answer 124**
**Strange Series**

If you don't believe this, hold the book up to a mirror. You will see that with the inclusion of the above, the numbers 1, 2, 3, 4, 5 appear in sequence.

**Answer 125**
**Sticky Business**
If the shorter pieces, placed end to end, are longer than the largest piece, then they will form a triangle.

**Answer 126**
**Fancy Figures**
Arrange them into groups of three, each totalling 1000.

457 + 168 + 375 = 1000

532 + 217 + 251 = 1000

349 + 218 + 433 = 1000

713 + 106 + 181 = 1000

**Answer 127**
**Unwanted Guest**
B.
It is a straight-sided figure within a curved figure.
The rest are curved figures within a straight
sided one.

**Answer 128**
**Following Fun**
D.
The small circle moves two on and one back. The
middle-size circle moves one back and two on. The
large circle moves one on and two back.

**Answer 129**
**Symbol Search**
B.

**Answer 130**
**Little and Large**
C. B and D, and A and E are the same, with large
and small circles reversed.